Can You Hear

The Holy Spirit?

Second Edition

PB Hawks

Printed in the United States of America
ISBN:0692446583

ASIN: B00N33PHXG:

DEDICATION

This book is dedicated to all Churchgoers so they can visualize the prominence of the Holy Spirit. See what is possible when the Holy Spirit is allowed to move freely in your Church.

ACKNOWLEDGMENTS

I am deeply proud of the teaching of my pastor, Dale Edwards. He has a way of saying something without speaking. He certainly reminds me of that old saying, "Preach the Gospel to all the world and use words only when necessary." Joe Sawicke is a dear friend who has been a huge help in editing this novel.

Table of Contents

Prologue

Prologue

I had a difficult time determining the title for this novel. I wanted the title to be a phrase that would describe the essence of the story. So I chose "Can You Hear The Holy Spirit?" The Holy Spirit has a sound that is very distinctive. Some may describe it as unknown tongue; others will say it captures their heart and others will have fear of the unknown.

Fear of the unknown makes us want or say things that we regret later on, so we take the approach of sending this unknown character away or try to hide from Him. We have, in many cases, assigned the Holy Spirit to oblivion ... a place in a far off land. You will find this story takes the Holy Spirit from this far off place and returns Him to His rightful place in the Church today.

The Church of Jesus Christ in recent years has made this assignment to the Holy Spirit. They have put Him in a far off place in an effort to silence Him. This has been going on, in large part, because of fear. Theirs certain traits that the Holy Spirit brings with Him that seem annoying to Church leaders. Speaking in an unknown tongue and a word of prophecy are two of the traits that some Church leaders can't handle.

The Church's difficulties happen because a number of its leaders have abused these traits and used them in an ungodly manner, the laying of hands to express one example. The Holy Spirit is all-powerful and doesn't need some Church leader to approach people to lay hands on them so they fall under the power of the Holy Spirit. This kind of showmanship has allowed for the fear that others have about the Holy Spirit. This is not consistent with the Holy Spirit; He is a gentle, kind person and does not want this kind of showmanship, although, I must say, the laying of hands, when done in the proper manner, gives the Holy Spirit an opportunity to bring spiritual health to many. If healing needs to happen then a simple asking and letting go and healing will take place as I have seen numerous times in my life. Church leaders don't have to force the Holy Spirit into healing or any of the other gifts that He gives freely. Church leaders must just believe and they will see miracles break out all around them. The Holy Spirit needs to be in control and that's not something they can live with. Control is vital to some Church leaders, which they will not release to the Holy Spirit. There are scores of excuses they use, like it might scare people away, but none of them make much sense.

The other aspect of the Holy Spirit that seems burdensome to many is speaking in an unknown tongue. The reason this is so perplexing is because they have had hands laid on them and they still can't speak in tongues. So they brush the Holy Spirit away, saying such things as, "If God wants me to have the Holy Spirit He will give Him to me," or "I don't think I need to speak in tongues." What they don't understand is God desires us to have this gift. So instead of giving up we need to seek Him until we find Him. When we are prayed for we must do our part. We must start saying something. The Holy Spirit doesn't speak for you ... you must speak for yourself. Start saying words or sounds and your pray language will come out. Some think that God is going to speak for them, no, you must do the speaking. Some most likely feel embarrassed so they don't speak out only to find some excuse to explain why they don't speak in tongues. In my previous book, The Visitor (which is still selling on Amazon), the Church in that small town had all their prayers answered after a stranger came to visit them and because they became ashamed of Him they hid Him in the basement and they lost everything. I suggest you obtain a copy and read the whole story for yourself.

The Holy Spirit is the person of the Godhead that was chosen to remain on Earth and be the strength to the new Church ... and the early Church understood what that meant. So they turned to Him to receive power that only He could give. They understood the words of Jesus and so did the devil. So our mortal enemy began an assault on this powerful person. As with all assaults, the results don't come all of sudden, but they come slowly and over an untold number of years, eventually moving from a church so integrated with the Holy Spirit to a Church trying to hide Him from the very people that need Him the most—the Church of Jesus Christ.

As you read you find two men so in love with Jesus that they want His Church to display the power Jesus displayed when He walked the earth. After all, didn't He promise us "We would do greater works?" So they wondered why they do not see this power in the Church of today. They did what anyone seeking this power would do, they prayed. They prayed intently trying to find the power of the Holy Spirit demonstrated in their church.

Anyone who has prayed to our heavenly Father knows the answer almost never comes the way you expect it to. In this town the answer came through an old woodsman. This old man responded to a request and helped produce an explosion of power not soon forgotten by the town's inhabitants. An explosion doesn't describe it very accurately, more like an avalanche of favor that continues to fall on that town.

Why does God show this kind of favor to a Church or town? Why are there so many other Churches or towns that need this favor and never receive it? God doesn't respond to a mere cry for help, but does respond to a cry that's full of faith and hope. We all have a need for some type of help, money, someone we love might be ill, or someone cries because of loneliness. These all require God to step in and help the one in need. All true believers should expect God to answer our prayers. However, let me express to you what I believe God wants to hear from His children. I think He wants to hear words that express belief in what He is all about. Let me show you what I mean.

"Father you are the God of all creation and you are the Great I AM. I have a need for money to pay off (name the bill you need to pay off). I thank you for the money that will come for this bill." There is a simple difference, but it may not be so simple when you need help.

It seems we ask God for something every time we talk to Him. Is it just me, or does it seem as though the only time we talk to God is when we want Him to do something for us? God wants a relationship with us and that means a dialogue between Him and us. Do we take the time to hear from God or does our relationship depend only upon Him answering our prayers? Some relationship, that is! If we want life to be happy, long and enjoyable, which is what God wants for us also, then we must seek Him in all we do.

We don't want Him only to be the one we ask for things we need. Is that what we want Him for? If that is what you want I don't think He is interested. Would you be? Have you ever had a friend who wanted you to do things for them all the time? Soon you decide you never want to talk him again. We think of God has that being that is high above us waiting for us to do something wrong so He can jump on us and correct us. That is so far from the truth, God is in love with us and wants to shower us with good things. He doesn't want to hurt us in any way.

If we want to see the favor of God upon your lives let's try to make Him a part of us, in everything we do. A true relationship with our loving God at the head is how we make Him part of our lives. So pray, He loves for us to pray, but take the time to talk to Him and not just ask for something. Then listen to His voice because He will answer you... Remember that still, small voice.

CHAPTER ONE – Shhh…Listen!

Living in Oregon gave Hank a sense of integrating with the environment. When he awakes and sees the wonder that surrounds him every day, he is overcome by the impressiveness that this State gives its residents. I don't know how you feel about the location where you reside, but Oregon gives its residents an appreciation of the beauty that is part of their everyday life. The beauty here is notoriously perplexing to describe. I just know that the residents of the State of Oregon are in awe most of the time. However, this comes with a burdensome price: during most of the fall, winter and some of the spring, the weather brings in the clouds and rain almost every day without stopping … at least it appears that way.

Having said this, I can't help but consider the glory of our God! His very Words brought the entire Universe and our planet Earth into existence! He loved us so abundantly that, for His pleasure, He shared His handiwork with the very people He created so that we could live with Him for all eternity. The exciting part of this is not only what we <u>can</u> see, but there is so much more that we <u>cannot</u> see and if we could just visualize the hidden benefits, it would 'boggle our minds'! God gave us the gift of 'Free Will' so that each of us could choose to be captured by the evil one or be liberated by His Glorious Goodness so we could enjoy all the awesome elements and facets of His creation!

Henry (Hank) Bent was born in a small town called Shadow in June 1975. His parents owned a modest farm about three miles north of this town. Hank grew up learning about farming and doing what most children do when living on a farm: he had chores to do before and after school. He was an average student and enjoyed being with his good friend Dean. The two of them did things that gave them an honorable although somewhat 'mischievous' reputation that the folks still remember to this day. Hank went to college and studied engineering, while Dean stayed on the farm until his Dad and Mom passed away. He sold the farm and was rewarded with a good amount of money. Dean went into business for himself and opened a hardware store in the middle of town. It soon became the best place to go to get whatever you needed and the best place to go to find out what was happening. Hank worked in the big city, just outside of Eugene, Oregon. At 35 years of age, he decided to move back home and teach. More about these two friends later... I'm getting a little ahead of myself.

One Sunday morning, after leaving the Church service, Hank and Dean went for breakfast to a little coffee shop south of town, something they did most Sundays. Hank was visibly dismayed and upset. When they were settled in their seats, Dean asked, "What's bothering you?"

Hank replied, "I'm tired of the lack of power in our Church!"

Dean then asked, "What brought that up?"

Hank's answer questioned why Churches today are not like the first century Churches, so Dean responded with "What do you mean?"

Hank's rejoinder was, "Weren't miracles taking place almost daily, and weren't there 'signs and wonders' demonstrated for all to see? How many miracles have you seen lately, and 'signs and wonders' for that matter?"

Hank concluded by saying, "The answer to these questions is…'none'!"

Dean and Hank both believe that God is the same today as He was then (see Hebrews 13:8). That being true, shouldn't His power be indistinguishable between 'then' and 'now?' "So… Why isn't it?" remarked Hank. "I've personally examined this question for some time and believe I've found the answer. I never believed man could do much on his own, unless there's a power behind him. There will be little or no substance in what he accomplishes without this power. Herein lies the dilemma our Churches face today: there's a deficiency of power and thus a myriad of people are losing out on their inheritance, which Jesus provided for us when He paid the price we couldn't pay: He died for our sins to redeem us and grant us salvation! Instead, we're losing out on the ability to heal in His name … losing out on the ability to share His love with the world. When others in the world look at us, do they see us living as they do … or do they see a people on fire, in love with a Savior who has given them freedom? Do they instead see us in love with a world that is dying without saving grace? The indisputable answer is: the world is dying all around us.

"To understand fully we must go back to the Cross. The Cross is where salvation originates and 'Good' starts. The Cross is where Jesus made all things new.

The Cross is where our eternity was changed and, through that one magnificent act, it brought us to what God wanted for us from the start. We lost it all by one man's disobedience ... but we gained it all back by one Man's act of love for us. What a simple statement and yet, all through the ages, it's lost its real meaning. It's quite simple: 'love' and 'relationship' are what matter ... not the 'rules' of the law. It's more like falling in love than just something to believe in. It's more like losing your heart than just giving your allegiance. Do you understand what I'm attempting to say?"

Dean said, "Yes! Look at what Jesus said in the Epistle of John, the fourteenth chapter:"

John 14:12-14
12 Most certainly I tell you, he who believes in Me, the works that I do, he will do also; and he will do greater works than these, because I am going to my Father.
13 Whatever you will ask in My name, that will I do, that the Father may be glorified in the Son.
14 If you will ask anything in My name, I will do it.

Acts 1:8
8 But you will receive power when the Holy Spirit has come upon you. You will be witnesses to Me in Jerusalem, in all Judea and Samaria, and to the uttermost parts of the earth."

"Did you hear what happened in that Church in Berry Town?" Hank asked.

"No, I didn't," replied Dean.

"Well, they said the Holy Spirit came to visit them. I was informed by some who were present that it transformed them for good and now they are seeing 'signs and wonders' at their Church!"

Dean interjected with "Do you believe that really happened? What do you mean 'the Holy Spirit came to visit them'?"

Hank responded, saying, "The way it was related to me was that a guy showed up at a Sunday morning service and, during introductions, was asked his name and he said it was 'H.S. Christian.' What transpired after that is extraordinary! The complete story is a little lengthy, but the end result made them a much more spiritual Church."

Dean calmly stated, "I doubt we could persuade the Holy Spirit to reach out to us, or perhaps God will send a word of some type... Do you think He would do that?"

Hank replied, "I know He loves us and wants only the best for us. It'll take a superabundant amount of faith and prayers... Are you up to it, Dean? I'm tired of going to a building each Sunday just to 'play church', aren't you?"

Dean said, "You know the answer to that! I too yearn for what the first Church did and the power that they exhibited! How do we get started?"

"I don't know... The only way I can think of is to pray every chance we get and never doubt anything as long as it lines up with the Scripture," Hank replied as he became more encouraged.

Dean's and Hank's Church, on the other hand, is modest in size and it is not where it should be spiritually. It is a loving, open-minded Church to a degree. It's had approximately 100 members since its inception, but is a gratifying place to worship and praise on Sunday mornings. The men have a Bible Study once a week and 15 to 20 participants attend it. When called to pray, the congregation meets in the sanctuary and Dean says they have a worship team that leads the singing and elevated praises to our Lord and Savior.

At one of the meetings, Dean began to describe how powerful the Holy Spirit had been in the Church over the years and how sad it is that this great power is no longer evident in today's Churches. The discourse that followed was very passionate. One of the arguments that was generated was, "The Baptism of the Holy Spirit is not a necessary requirement for salvation." True as this may be, it was very important to Jesus and the Father. Jesus made it very clear that it is essential that He go to the Father so the Holy Spirit could come and be our Helper. This being true, why is the Holy Spirit so neglected in the Church today? Isn't it obvious that Jesus' and the Father's precept is that the receiving of the Holy Spirit is not an option and, therefore, the Baptism of the Holy Spirit is essential for the establishment and the success of the Church?

This small country Church faces numerous obstacles, similar to so many Churches today. The need for a new roof, pews that are worn and need replacing, a sound system that is well beyond repair and new classrooms are just a few of the paramount items that need attending to. An absence of any notable increase in tithes and offerings can also be added to this list—a challenge that has not been met since this Church's initial inauguration. Of paramount importance, however, is the need for 'spiritual awakening' that defies description.

It has always amazed me how anyone can continue to do the same things in the same way even though the outcome isn't what they desire. I understand that 'change' is difficult even for the eldest of us. However, there is a time when we must take a vigorous look at what is being accomplished, if anything, and make accommodations. Somehow, Churches don't seem to think that this applies to them. So, year after year, some Churches do nothing different and their accomplishments always seem to remain the same. Can't they see that without the Holy Spirit they have no power to do anything substantial for the Lord? It makes one conclude that they just don't seem to care— and that possibility becomes more and more evident. Can the Church really go year after year and look at the Word without considering the Holy Spirit? I surmise that the 'tongues stuff' is too much for them and they will do anything to avoid the Holy Spirit … even if it means not following scripture.

When Hank was very young, he visualized God as an old man who was 'in control' and one had to answer to Him when one did wrong—and he did wrong most of the time (at least that's what he was told). He acknowledged Jesus as his Creator and the One who died for him, and he always loved and thanked Him for all He did. However, the Holy Spirit was one person of the Godhead that he knew virtually nothing about, and that circumstance continued until he asked Jesus into his heart. At that time, the Holy Spirit became a 'real person' to him because He was so instrumental in his conversion. As he began to immerse himself in the scriptures, the Holy Spirit became more alive each day. Today, in most of our Churches, the Holy Spirit is mentioned very infrequently, if at all. Nevertheless, the Holy Spirit is the solution to so many of our problems. Yes, with this indispensable gift that the Father desires us to obtain, the Church will be the 'head' and not the 'tail'. But instead of embracing Him, they reject Him … instead of receiving Him as a blessing, they are ashamed of Him … and instead of celebrating Him, they hide from Him and speak of Him as an 'it'. Does this sound like your Church?

CHAPTER TWO HANK REMINISCES…

I mentioned previously that Hank was raised in the small town of Shadow, Oregon, and returned from his engineering career to teach in the local school. He taught English, Math, History and Speech. He is a good teacher and his students enjoy their time in his classroom. However, when he attended college, his tenure there was a little wild and loose. He and his fellow classmates partied and drank alcoholic beverages a bit too much. His grades were average and he went with college girls that were as 'loose' as he was. To Hank, Christianity was a far-out concept and he wouldn't have anything to do with it. How could a 'party-guy' like he was turn around and embrace a life of being a Christian? Little did he know that the Holy Spirit was moving through an outstanding woman!

Her name was Donna Wells and she goes to Grace Christian Church. Donna had a wonderful childhood with the most amazing parents. She was taught the Word of God before she able to walk. School before college was excellent. She stayed away from friends who would demean her Christian walk. She entered college with a strong spirit, which allowed her to keep her faith in Jesus Christ.

Hank went with friends to a football practice; it so happened that the cheerleaders were also practicing. That's when Hank got his first look at Donna, and his first impression was: how could anyone be so beautiful? He set his sights on meeting her. His friends told him not to mess with her because of her Christianity. Hank was determined, and sought out friends who knew her so they could introduce him. He had no luck until he went to a baseball game and found himself sitting just a few seats away from where Donna was sitting.

His excitement got the best of him and he moved close to her and introduced himself. "Hi! My name is Hank."

She looked at him and said, "Yes! I know… You have quite a reputation around campus."

Hank responded, "I'm not as bad as they say. I'd like to get to know you better."

Donna replied, "The only way that's going to happen is if you attend one our Church gatherings."

Hank was not about to attend some church gathering, that would have been too far-out for him. So he smiled and said, "Maybe some other time, thank you."

He was then surprised to hear her say, "OK, if you change your mind, we are located on G Street … about the middle of the block. Oh! About 7:00 pm on Tuesday. I do hope I see you there."

Wow! He couldn't believe the feeling he was experiencing. He could get any girl he wanted, so why was he feeling this way? The game was over and Donna left with her friends, but gave him a 'look' before she took off.

He decided to go out with the guys and party. It was Saturday night and there were plenty of women he could make it with, he thought. Nevertheless, he couldn't party that night, instead, he found himself walking around campus thinking about his reputation and what people might be saying about him. He started to think about his life and what it had become. He thought about Donna and how beautiful she was and how his reputation could end his chances of getting to know her better. Here it was a Saturday night and he was alone feeling sorry for what he had become up until now. He decided to go to the gathering on Tuesday night. Why? He had no idea. Something inside was drawing him to go.

Tuesday night finally arrived and the moon in the sky was as big as Hank had ever observed before. It shined so bright that one could almost drive without headlights. He was on his way to the Grace Christian Church with one thought on his mind—to see a beautiful girl named Donna. What, was he nuts? Never did he think he would be entering a church building. He was raised without God or any Church on Sundays.

Donna noticed him enter and went over to him. "I'm glad you could make it," she said.

Hank then led the conversation with, "What do you people do at these meetings?"

Donna, somewhat startled, said, "You people... What does that mean?"

Hank picked up on her 'angst' and said, "I'm sorry, I didn't mean it in any hurtful way."

Donna confidently said, "I'm sure you didn't."

Hank searched for the right words and said, "I'm afraid I started off badly... Can we begin again?"

So Donna quickly forgave him and said, "What we do is honor our God ... a God who was willing to die on a cross so we could be free; a God so in love with us that He sent his only Son so we could become his adopted children."

Hank recovered from his temporary embarrassment and said, "I never heard it put that way before. I guess the love of God has never been made known to me."

Donna continued with, "His name is Jesus ... and, Hank, He loves you more than you will ever know. He is extending His hand to you right now and is asking you to believe in Him."

Hank responded, "Donna, I'm feeling something I can't explain. It's a sense of love and I feel it all over me."

Donna then said, "That's the Holy Spirit, Hank. You see, I've been praying for you."

Hank didn't know what to say. He had never felt the love of God before. Was this true or was he experiencing something cooked up by Donna? He thought, *Is this real?* The only answer had to be yes it is! "Donna, what should I do?"

Donna followed with the right answer: "Ask Jesus into your life."

Hank's next question was, "How do I do that?"

Donna's answer: "Go somewhere special and ask God to show you what to do."

At that point, Hank just ran out of the building and drove back to his room. *That was a bunch of nonsense!* he thought. *I'm just going to get some sleep. How could God love me? I'm nothing special, I didn't even go to church once in my life.*

Hank and Donna soon became an item. Donna agreed to go on a date with Hank even though he didn't come to any of her church meetings. They spent a great deal of time together during the summer months. They went on camping outings with friends; they went to the coast and slept on the beach. They even took climbing lessons and took a shot at climbing a local mountain. The attempt only took them half the way up the mountain, but the sights were breathtaking. They were falling in love with each other and he couldn't remember a better time in his whole life. He never knew what love felt like but he couldn't get her out of his mind.

Just before graduation arrived, Donna and her friends planned to go to a Hank Williams concert. Donna was informed that she finished tops in her class; Hank knew he was 'average' as always. He didn't care so much about his grades; his love for Donna was paramount in his mind. Donna, on the other hand, was more concerned about Hank's relationship with God. She knew she could not marry a man who hadn't asked Jesus into his life. Her love for Hank would take second place to her love for Jesus.

The weekend the girls decided to go to see Hank Williams in concert, the car they thought they were taking broke down, so Hank let them use his car. The concert was approximately a hundred miles away so they decided they would stay in a small motel and return back to campus that Monday. As life would have it, they were hit with one of those monster rainstorms that caught them by surprise. The rain and the wind were so powerful that they had to turn into the first motel they came to. The motel was on the way and not far from the concert location.

During the night, three men broke into their room and, at gunpoint, raped them, including Donna. The girls were found the next morning—two were injured very badly and Donna was close to death. The scene in that motel room was one of complete horror! The girls were naked and bleeding. Donna was beaten severely, her eyes were swollen and almost shut. There were scars all over her face, neck and chest. It seems she did everything in her power to prevent the others from being raped so she took most of the beating.

Hank heard what had happened, asked his friend for the use his car and rushed to the hospital and to Donna's bedside. He was broken to see her in this condition. Bandages covered her face and arms and that is what you could see, what about the wounds on the inside that couldn't be seen? With tears pouring from his eyes, he took her hand. She looked at him with those beautiful blue eyes and said, "Pray with me."

He said, "How could you pray to a God who would allow this to happen?"

She said, "Hank, I love you… Don't blame God for this. He was with me all through this ordeal. He never let me go. He was holding me in His arms. Hank, you need to accept Him into your life or you will lose out for all eternity and I don't want that for you."

He was amazed that she was thinking of him at this time. He was overwhelmed with love for her, but all he could do was cry. She looked at Hank for the last time before she closed her eyes and withdrew from this life forever. Hank took her in his arms and cried with mourns that could be heard on the whole floor as he held her for what seemed like hours before her mother and father arrived. Even though he never met them before, he loved them because of what Donna had told him about them and they seemed to know him as well. They cried together and consoled each other and each said their goodbyes to their beautiful, beloved Donna.

Hank went back to his schooling and, after graduation, he was accepted by a large engineering firm in Eugene, Oregon. He had nothing except the job to occupy his mind. The nights were the hardest times … he could not stop thinking about Donna. He cursed God many times, which didn't help his condition of grief. He was so broken and couldn't get her out of his mind. *How could a beautiful woman like Donna leave this world in such an awful way? How can I live without her grace?* were amongst the thoughts that continually ran through Hank's mind.

It has been a number of years since he lost Donna, and thinking about her is still very painful. He's now going to a small Church in Eugene. His heart hurt for so long and he wanted to feel better, but he didn't know how. He then remembered Donna's words "…don't lose out on eternity." His anger with God had come to an end months ago. On his knees in his bedroom, he cried out and said, "God, I'm hurting and broken. I need You, Lord. I need to know You more. Forgive me for all my wrong- doings. I know You died on a cross for me and rose from the dead to set me free, and You live today. Come into my life and make me new". He fell on his face and cried to the point of exhaustion. He slept the whole night through ... something that had not happened for numerous months.

He awoke to a sunny day and felt as if a heavy weight had been lifted off of his entire being. It was as if he was 'new' in every way. There was even a smile on his face. After plenty of consideration, he decided to leave his engineering position and return home. "Perhaps I could teach," he said softly.

CHAPTER THREE – DEAN THINKS
BACK TO...

Farms were plentiful in this area. Most had sheep and some cattle; a few had horses. Yet the farms that brought in the most money were the ones that provided food, such as corn, milk, and produce of all kinds. Dean's first recollection of his childhood was working in the fields with his dad. He was only seven but his dad needed workers so Dean became his dad's farm hand. That's how he was treated, just like a farm hand not a son, for most of his life. That was hard for a seven-year-old to understand. He was given chores to do morning and evening after school. School was difficult for Dean because he had homework that he had to do and the only time he could get it done was after supper. The chores had to be done every day (including Saturday and Sunday), while homework was only during the weekdays. The excitement of 'living' for a young boy on a farm, I should say for a young boy on this farm, was not exciting at all. It was downright hard and lonesome. Dean's family worked all the time with no outlet for having fun.

When he entered high school, he didn't have many friends, except for Hank. The two spent a great deal of time with each other when they could. Hank was the only one who Dean could share anything with, including his plans to run away. They became the kids to be mindful of in town because they pulled so many pranks on anyone they could experiment with. One day they took the Wilsons' tractor and somehow they made a way to lift it up onto the roof of Mr. Wilson's barn.

The town is still talking about it today. Truth was they had a friend who worked on a nearby farm who put together a rig that could lift up anything. At one time they told all the kids in town that the government was printing new three-dollar bills and they knew how to get them first. They would print the three-dollar bills on their computer and buy some special paper to print the new bills on. When you looked at them, they were as good as a real bill. There were a lot more pranks that they pulled off. It soon became apparent that you couldn't believe anything they said.

Dean's mother and father were not a loving or caring couple. Sometimes they were downright mean. He dreamed of leaving and never coming back, but where and how he would eat or sleep he could never quite figure out, so life continued in the same way after graduation from High School ... until his dad died. Dean was about twenty-five years old by this time. His mother was not doing well and two months after his father's death, she passed away. For the first time, Dean was in control, so the first thing he did was sell the farm. He wanted it sold, and he didn't care how much he received for the place. There were rumors that a multi-million dollar offer was made, which Dean accepted. He was free of that place and free from the memories that haunted him. It turns out that he had endured physical and mental abuse for far too many years.

Dean went on a long vacation—Europe, Asia, Japan– then came back to the States. He arrived in California and drove up the western coast until Oregon was in his sight. He didn't have any women in his life, but I know many who would give almost anything to get involved with him. So Dean became very selective. He was determined to find only the right one. He was home for about six months when a beautiful woman came into his life. Her name was Shellie, red hair, blue eyes and about 5'-3". She was everything he hoped a wife would be, and more. They spent a great deal of time together. Dean helped her find a house and showed her all of the State of Oregon. He asked her to marry him and three months later they were married in the town's Christian Church. She became the town's Liberian after Mrs. Myers retired.

Dean was enamored with this town called Shadow and even though it carried destructive memories when was growing up, as long as he stayed away from the farm he would be OK. He purchased a large shop... No, it was several shops on Ocean Street in the heart of town. He turned them into a hardware store. It wasn't 'just' a hardware store, it was the <u>best</u> hardware store in a fifty-mile area. He sold everything from the smallest screw to the kitchen sink. It became the area's most popular place to be. People came to walk through it just to see the items he sold and it became the town's biggest attraction. He didn't have to work because he had all the money he needed, but he loved being there and meeting the local townspeople every day.

When Hank returned to town, their friendship picked up right where it left off. Hank began to discuss the Lord with Dean, telling him about the love of the Lord and how much Jesus loved him. This was extremely new to Dean because he couldn't remember anyone ever loving him, except for his new bride. They would deliberate for hours about the Bible and its contents. Dean was convinced that the Bible was either a total joke or a compilation of the most profound writings he had ever read.

Hank led his friend to the Lord one dark, rainy night. They prayed together and spent time in the Word of God. Dean said, "What an experience! The feeling of love from the Lord is unmistakable! How come I never felt this before?"

"Because you made a commitment this time," Hank told him.

CHAPTER FOUR

A REMOTE ENCOUNTER…

Oregon possesses numerous amounts of lakes and forests that cover nearly all of the land. Some of these lakes are close to civilization where access is easy; others are remote and very difficult to find and even more demanding to search out. In one of these very remote locations lived an old woodsman named Jedd. The one-room cabin he lives in is old and rugged and has been home for Jedd for almost thirty years. Jedd occupied this cabin soon after a drunk driver killed his wife and his two children. Jedd's life was doing well before the car crash. He had just become an ordained minister with the 'Assembly of God'. He was applying for a position of pastor in a small Church in the northern part of Oregon. He put in many hours to obtain this ministry and was looking forward to spending time with his family, until that unforgettable day. He could not go on; he thought of suicide but couldn't get the courage to it. He wandered through Oregon before selecting this place to settle down.

Becoming an integral member of the woods for that length of time… Well, to say that Jedd is 'out of the ordinary' is a gross understatement! Jedd's days are filled with gardening, fishing, reading his Bible and communicating with God; and, yes, it does seem he's out there … all by his lonesome. Now, before we start thinking that Jedd is some kind of 'screwball' or a 'psycho', it is a life that we may not understand, but it is a life that Jedd selected and he's happy living this way. 'Speaking to God' is not as unusual as you may imagine. Don't we pray when we want God to do something that we consider important to us? Is that not speaking to God? Our problem, unlike Jedd's circumstance, is that there's so much that distracts us from hearing God. In the quiet of Jedd's remote site, hearing God is not so mystifying. During his years in the woods, angels have visited Jedd and the Lord has revealed countless wonders. Jedd is a man who doesn't need a great deal to satisfy him, so when the Lord asks him to do something for Him, Jedd accepts without question.

A Conversation with God...

In recent days, during a conversation with the Almighty, Jedd was asked if he would do something for Him. Jedd's immediate response was, "What is it, Lord?" Jedd then understood Him to say, "I want you to visit a small town and a Church to reveal to them a gift that I've wanted them to have for some time. This gift will give them abilities they never dreamed possible and will bring them knowledge they never believed they could obtain. Tell them I have heard their prayers and will answer them." Jedd was somewhat startled by this request, but agreed to take on the mission.

Still perplexed by the assignment, Jedd pondered the question: How could he go into the world again after all these years? Jedd's lifestyle allowed him not to shave for countless years, which enabled him to grow quite a long beard. "Do I shave, what kind of clothes do I wear ... and how long will this take to complete? Lord, what are the answers to these questions?"

The Lord replied, "It makes no difference what you wear; but you can buy clothes in a local shop and trim your facial hair. Your journey will take you about a week just to get to the main road. However, you will spend time with the people of this Church, for you will lead them into the Truth and I will bless them."

Jedd went to the lake and washed his clothes and hung them on a tree branch to dry. He packed a backpack and knocked the mud off his boots then polished them with water. After his clothes had dried and his packing was complete, he knelt to pray before he began his journey. He prayed for health, wisdom, and protection and thanked God for trusting him to achieve a good outcome to this assignment. Getting out from his home-site proved to be arduous and, at times, the woods seemed impenetrable. He made his way through brush that almost beat him up! He encountered fallen trees, some the size of a large truck. It took him a whole week just to find a road that truly was considered a road … a road that led somewhere; a road where traffic proceeded in both directions. As God directed, Jedd walked toward the small town. Someone stopped to ask where he was going and Jedd pointed in the direction of the small town up ahead. The driver said, "Hop in and I'll take you there." Jedd's journey was well under way and the townspeople had no idea what was about to transpire!

After shopping for some clothes in a nearby thrift shop, he found a modest motel and secured a room to sleep in for the night. The room was nothing to speak about, but Jedd lay down and began to think about what he was supposed to do when he arrived at 'Sunday Service' the next day. As he reflected about his visit, he drifted off to sleep. He awoke to a bright, cheerful, sunny day. Truly "…this is a day the Lord had made, rejoice and be glad in it!"(Psalm 118:24) When he was finished dressing, he went to the lobby to get a cup of coffee. He didn't have any money when he started his journey, but when he put his hand in his pocket, he found a sufficient supply of dollars! He paid for his room for another night and wondered why he didn't pay for a longer stay. He then realized immediately that "...the Lord is in control. I'll follow where he leads me." So he proceeded down the road to the Church.

The Church was small, as anticipated, with a quaint old charm to it. It was painted white with majestic stained glass windows and a bell tower—the kind of Church you would expect to see in some vintage paintings. It excited Jedd but he didn't really know why. It had been a multitude of years since he'd seen or entered a building of such noble stature. Jedd began to remember the agonizing circumstances that shepherded him away from the life that these townspeople were living. He hadn't considered just how painful this mission might become. However, Jedd loved God so much that he said 'yes' even though he hadn't realized what he might be getting himself into.

The spring sunlight created a surreal 'sparkle' to the building ... something like a vision of the Crystal Cathedral ... truly something to behold! Jedd, along with the rest of the congregation, entered and Jedd was greeted with warm 'hello's and hand-shakes from the men. He sat in the back row and nobody paid much attention to him except for an infrequent greeting by those who surrounded him.

The church service began with worship songs and praise to our Lord. Then, all of a sudden, Jedd began to sing, and what we heard astounded us beyond description! The sound was exquisite ... but 10 times louder than anyone else! To some it even hurt their ears! The worship ended earlier than was customary and most were thankful for that. The remainder of the service went on as normally as could be expected. The people were leaving the building and the pastor acknowledged all who were exiting with, "Thank you for coming," and a handshake. When he greeted Jedd, he said, " You sing with a thunderbolt kind of voice!"

Jedd replied with, "I love praising the Lord and, where I come from, I sing as loud as I can."

"Yes," said the pastor, "but here we try to sing with everyone in one accord."

Jedd responded with, "Yes, pastor... I'll keep that in mind."

New Living Accommodations...

One of the women then inquired as to where Jedd was staying and he responded, "In a modest motel down the street." The woman said she had an empty room above her garage and he was welcome to have it as long as he liked. Jedd thanked the woman and indicated that he would love to see it.

The woman (whose name was Ann) said, "Come with me and I'll show it to you." So they walked a few blocks and soon stood before a big, old mansion that was splendid in every way! After living in a one-room cabin for so many years, Jedd was elated! She led him to a huge building that was detached from the main house and she called it 'the garage'. To Jedd, this was no 'garage'! Her offer was an outstanding gesture by a loving woman. They went up a flight of stairs and entered a room with a kitchen on one side, a living space on the other and a door to the right side that he perceived would lead to the bedroom. Jedd could not believe that she offered this fabulous place for him to stay! He was so thankful that he volunteered to do any work she needed to be done. She said, "Perhaps one day, but for now just take some time to relax and get settled in."

He said, "Ann, would you pray with me?" Jedd gave thanks to the Lord for his new accommodations and asked Him to bless this wonderful woman.

Jedd went to the Church the following day, but was informed that it was the pastor's day-off. This gave him time to look around and notice numerous tasks that he could start on when the pastor gave the 'OK'. The following day, he and the pastor went over the items that Jedd observed and he was given the pastor's blessing to do whatever he thought was necessary. Jedd started immediately and spent most of the day working around the Church, all the while still asking God what He wanted him to do! The Lord said, "You're doing just fine." Jedd was somewhat confused but said nothing and continued working around the Church.

Sunday arrived again and it was another noteworthy day. All of the parishioners entered the Church and took their seats, while Jedd sat in the very back row as he did the first day he arrived. The singing and praise began and Jedd again sang with the loudest voice you ever heard! Even though the people had heard him before, his voice was still 'shocking' to the ears! Soon the singing stopped and the rest of the service was just great. I would like to tell you that Jedd's voice was lower in the future services, but it was not. However, there was something uniquely different and surprising: the congregation all started to sing a little louder each Sunday! It became refreshing and gave them freedom to sing without worrying about how they sounded. A new spirit of 'joy' began to infiltrate the Church and that previous 'tense feeling' mentioned earlier slowly went away.

The Beginning Effects of the Holy Spirit...

Since Jedd started coming to Sunday services, 'giving' of tithes and offerings actually increased to the point that the Church could begin to afford things previously put 'on-hold', such as installing a new roof on the Church (something that absolutely needed to be done). They even started planning the replacement of the seating and the upgrading of the sound system. What was happening? No one seemed to know the reason, nor did anyone want it to stop! Jedd completed all the 'pastor-approved-work' and a whole lot more. He soon became indispensable and before long he knew more about the church building and its grounds than anyone else. One day, the pastor said, "Jedd, we have a problem... Our Sunday school teacher is very ill and he won't be back for several weeks. How about teaching his class? I have no one else."

Jedd thought for a moment, and then asked, "Could I teach on any subject I want?"

"Yes, you may," was the pastor's response.

Jedd said, "Then I would be honored!" So began a series of events that would rattle the Church's core!

Jedd Begins To Teach...

The day came when Jedd would instruct his first Sunday school class. The expectancy was great. Some were curious to see what this woodsman would teach them and why the pastor would let him take over the class. The pastor introduced Jedd to them with enthusiasm and appreciation. He said Jedd had a great deal to teach based on so many varied experiences, which had brought him to their Church. So Jedd took 'center-stage' and began to tell about his background, his upbringing … that he was raised in Eastern Oregon where he lived and how he now lives in a little island in Shadow Lake and now, because of his location, was able to commune with God daily. Jedd recounted why he settled on the lifestyle that allowed him to be alone and close to nature.

He mentioned the dreadful event that brought him to this lifestyle, without going into details. He said he wanted to be in a place where he could hear the voice of God. He desired to be away from anything that may distract him from being in God's presence. There were some in the class who wanted to know more, but Jedd indicated that he himself was not part of the Sunday school subject matter, but would gladly make himself available to answer any questions at a later time.

"The main subject of our class today (and for perhaps several weeks) will be the Holy Spirit. I want to start by emphasizing that you need to forget everything you've ever been 'taught, heard or think-you-know' about the Holy Spirit because of prior teachings you may have had that are erroneous and inappropriate… So I want to 'level the playing field'. The Holy Spirit will lead us and guide us through this class. You will experience His presence and He will touch your hearts and minds. Every class will start off by asking the Holy Spirit to take control of what will be said and to provide you with answers to your questions. So with that said, let's begin."

CHAPTER FIVE – THE HOLY SPIRIT…

Jedd instructed the class to "Turn, in your Bibles, to **John 14:12-17**.

12 "Most assuredly I tell you, he who believes in Me, the works that I do, he will do also; and he will do greater works than these, because I am going to My Father.

13 "Whatever you will ask in My name, that will I do, that the Father may be glorified in the Son.

14 "If you ask anything in My name, I will do it.

15 "If you love Me, keep My commandments.

16 "I will pray to the Father, and He will give you another Helper, that He may abide with you forever —

17 "The Spirit of truth, whom the world cannot receive, for it neither sees Him nor knows Him; but you know Him, for He dwells with you, and will be in you.

"That's a pretty substantial piece of scripture! Let's look at these words closely and truly comprehend what Jesus is saying to the world. The first is 'belief'. If we 'believe in Him and the works that He does, we will do greater works'. What! We are going to do greater works than Jesus our Lord? How can that be? Jesus explains this by saying, 'because He is going to His Father'. Then He continues to tell us that 'if we ask anything in His name, He will do it so His Father may be glorified'. He then asks us to 'love Him and keep His commandments'. Was He speaking about the Ten Commandments? No! He was speaking about the commandment to 'love God with all your heart and love your neighbor as yourself.' Now comes the part that most Christians get wrong.

"Let me speak to you straight: the 'Spirit of truth' that Jesus is expressing is the Holy Spirit. He is someone that the world doesn't know, but 'you know Him because He dwells in you.' Yes! When we ask Jesus into our lives, the Holy Spirit comes to dwell in us. Let's take a look at Acts 1:8 which shows us there is more to the Holy Spirit than just His indwelling.

Acts 1:8
8 "But you will receive power when the Holy Spirit has come upon you; and you shall be witnesses to Me in Jerusalem, in all Judea and Samaria, and to the uttermost parts of the earth.

"Now Jesus isn't talking about the 'indwelling of the Holy Spirit.' He says 'when the Spirit has come upon you.' Do you see the difference? Let's say the Holy Spirit takes the form of water. We fill up a glass with water and drink it all. Now the water (Holy Spirit) is in you, right? What if we had a pool filled with water and we jump in? Now the water is 'upon' us … and we are 'in' the water (Holy Spirit). Do you decipher what I am saying? I repeat: We now are 'in' the Holy Spirit. This is extremely significant. The necessity to tell the difference between 'indwells' and 'upon' will usher us into 'the truth'. There is something else that is immensely essential and that is the 'reason' for the Holy Spirit to come 'upon' us. It is that we might 'receive power'. Without the Holy Spirit 'upon' us, we will have no power to accomplish anything for God…neither Power to spread the Gospel or witness to the entire known world. Do you think the Church of Jesus Christ could have made the advances it did without the Holy Spirit? The answer is obvious. Then why does the Christian Church think it can do anything worthwhile for God without His Spirit today?

"Are you 'baptized in the Holy Spirit' (i.e. has the Holy Spirit come upon you)? In other words, are you 'immersed' in the Holy Spirit? Some say that they don't need to be immersed in the Holy Spirit (Baptized in the Holy Spirit) because they already received the Holy Spirit when they accepted Jesus Christ as their Savior and that in itself is enough for the rest of their lives. Some possibly look at others who say they are 'filled' with the Holy Spirit (Baptized in the Holy Spirit) but bear little fruit in their Christian lives; and so they say, 'If that's the result of being filled with the Holy Spirit, better not to have that Spirit at all.'

"To clarify these points, let's look to the Bible for the answers. I'm hopeful that this analysis assures you of the 'need' for the 'Baptism in the Holy Spirit.' Being 'filled' is something all believers receive when they've opened the door of their hearts and asked Jesus to be their Lord and Savior. At that point, we've become 'temples' of the Holy Spirit. However, just like the disciples 'waited,' we have to 'wait' for the Holy Spirit to come … even though Jesus 'breathed' on them in order that they 'receive' the Holy Spirit." (See John 20:22).

Miracles Begin to Happen...

Jedd then said, "OK! That will do it for today, but I don't want you to go without asking the Holy Spirit to do something for just one of you. Is there anyone who needs a touch from God?"

A middle-aged woman stood and said, "Jedd, my son John has a rare illness that is going to kill him. The doctors don't know what they can do to save him. He's gone through so many tests, blood drawn almost every hour. I don't know how long he can endure all this."

Jedd spoke these words: "Dear Father, we come before You in the name of Your Son, Jesus Christ. For 'by His stripes, we are healed!' Thank you, Father, for this miracle in John's life ... and may You be glorified! Amen. See you all next week."

The class left the Sunday School, which is located just to the west of the Church building, entered the Church and began taking their seats, saying 'hello' and greeting all who weren't at Sunday School ... when, all of a sudden, a cell phone sounded and a great cry went out from the very woman Jedd had just prayed for! The parishioners were startled as she cried out and said, "The doctors just informed my husband that John was healing! They started to examine him and his blood pressure was stable and his vital signs looked much better! John is 'on-the-mend' and gaining strength! About two hours ago, they thought he was going to die, but something made them go back and re-examine him! They found that he was recovering and the doctors don't know how this was happening! Thank You, God! And thanks to all in our Sunday school for praying!" The congregation all began rejoicing and praising the Lord! What a way to start Sunday Services!

Loving The Needy...

The next week can only be described as 'sensational'! The sun shined radiantly and brought with it the fragrance of summer. The congregation was blessed with the knowledge of knowing the Holy Spirit was showing their Church His goodness.

Jedd began his week working around the churchyards ... cutting grass, trimming trees and bushes and planting flowers. The grounds of the Church never looked so beautiful! Jedd was also told of the need to reach out to the homeless, so he collected blankets and clothes for them. He also was informed that the homeless didn't hang around town, but persisted in being in the adjacent wooded areas. So Jedd started to walk with the load of goods and someone said, "You can't walk to them carrying such a load, let me drive you."

Jedd said, "OK, but first can we stop at the local food bank and pick up some provisions to distribute when we get there?"

It wasn't long before they found several people in need and, after a few hours, all the goods and clothing were distributed. Jedd then asked his driver/helper if he knew of any others needing assistance. He made a list of the suggestions given to him and they went back to town. Later that week, they also visited the poor and widows in the town and handed out food from the food bank to them as well.

Someone in town was ailing with a stroke and asked for Jedd to come and pray with them at the hospital. Ben is a man in his early fifties and married to his wife for twenty-five years. He has his own construction company and was at work when the stroke hit him. Near the bed were his wife Grace and his children, Jan and Mary (14 & 15 years old, respectively). The four of them held hands, for they all loved God, and began to pray.

Jedd laid hands on the husband, Ben, and prayed, saying, "We come in the name of Your Son Jesus, Father. You are a great God who loves us deeply! Father, be glorified in this healing and may Ben magnify Your Name in all that he does, Amen."

Ben began to feel better immediately! The day after, he was walking and speaking without any evidence of the stroke! WOW! This miracle was a sign that the Spirit of the living God was visiting their town!

Receiving The Holy Spirit...

Sunday arrived again with a joy and peace that was felt by all. The congregation started to pray and Jedd began Sunday school with a review from the week before. "Last week, we talked about how much Jesus and the Father want us to have the gift of the Holy Spirit and the Baptism of the Holy Spirit. We also learned about 'why' it is so important to receive this gift. Without this influential power, we will not be able to succeed in anything worthwhile for Jesus. So let's get started on this week's session!

"How do we get the Baptism of the Holy Spirit?" someone shouted.

"Good question! Rather than give you the steps to take, let's understand that God doesn't give this gift just because you 'ask' for it. He gives you this gift because you 'desire' it above all things! To best make sense of this, let's look into our past and remember when we wanted something so much it would keep us up at night just thinking of how good it would be to posses it! That's what God wants from us ... and that takes time to reflect on the 'need' for the Holy Spirit or the 'reason' for Him ... so we must take the time to do just that! The Father loves us so much that He wants us to 'possess' the Baptism of the Holy Spirit! The question is: do we love Him enough to want this gift for ourselves? This means that we must search our hearts and minds and develop an insatiable desire for Him!"

Looking Closer...

"Let's look closer at the Holy Spirit and see what the benefits are of being baptized in Him. We are talking about the same Holy Spirit that came upon Jesus at His water Baptism and the same Spirit that began Jesus' ministry. This is the same Holy Spirit that raised Jesus from His tomb, the same Holy Spirit that came upon the disciples on the day of Pentecost when 3,000 people were saved, and the same Holy Spirit that gave the disciples the power to start the Christian Church! As we remember, when the Word was preached, 'signs and wonders' followed. That's the power that we are talking about and the power that's needed in the Church today!

"The main purpose of the Baptism in the Holy Spirit in this life, then, is to give us more of His power to demonstrate who Christ is and to assure people of His existence in this day and age, so they can be saved

(Acts 1:8) and spend eternity with Him in Heaven. All other things being equal, the believer Baptized in the Spirit will have more success in preaching the Gospel, because the Holy Spirit is free to work through him. The Holy Spirit has many ways to influence people: He gives us power to heal the sick and cast out demons (Mark 16:17, 18), so that people can see that Jesus is 'alive' and that His salvation is real and that He makes an incredible difference in our lives! It is much easier to lead people to Christ after they have been healed through Christ's power (which is often done, for example, by the 'laying-on-of-hands' by one or more Spirit-filled believers).

"With the Holy Spirit working through many believers, there are greater possibilities for the effective presentation of the Gospel (i.e. 'Good News') of the Kingdom than there were in the days of Jesus' earthly ministry. The Baptism in the Spirit, therefore, is an essential ingredient in the 'Eternal Plan' of God… The intent of this Plan is to multiply Jesus' earthly ministry of preaching, healing and casting out demons so that He can touch the whole world with its billions of people!"

Then it was time once again to pray for someone in need. An older man rose and said that the doctors told him his heart could not be repaired and he wanted Jedd to pray for him.

Jedd said, "I have no great power of my own, so only in the name of Jesus will I pray for you." So Jedd went over to this man and prayed these words: "I come in the name of Jesus and lay hands on my brother in Christ and ask that his heart be made new and that the Father may be glorified and His will be done! Amen!"

The man fell to the floor and everyone panicked, then someone called 911! The members of the class were all shocked, but soon the paramedics came and took him to the hospital. That was not the reaction expected, of course, so an additional prayer was said for him! Then the service began in the usual fashion … and when it was over, the parishioners began to exit the Church. Jedd was asked what had happened, so he started to explain about the man who was taken to the hospital by the paramedics, when the man came running to the pastor and Jedd yelling, "Guys! The doctors checked me out and said my health is like a man 20 years younger than me! Pastor! Jedd! I've been healed by the power of God! Hallelujah!"

Everyone started rejoicing right there outside the Church! Jedd asked what happened and the man said he was taken to the hospital and he felt fine but they put him through the tests that they normally do and the results were perfect! He said, "The doctors and nurses were so surprised and couldn't understand what had happened! I told them that God Himself has touched me and I will never be the same!"

CHAPTER SIX

IMMERSED IN THE H0LY SPIRIT...

Monday began with the fog still lingering in the upper part of the trees and the sun just breaking through the clouds. *I wonder how the people in the town feel about what is happening with all the miracles taking place ... or have they even noticed?* Hank and Dean met for coffee and Hank knew the miracles didn't get past Dean. Hank said, "How much do you know about Jedd, our Sunday School teacher?"

Dean replied, "Not much."

Hank continued, "It's getting really interesting! Tell me, Dean, you attended the Sunday school when Jedd was teaching. Do you believe that the Father and Jesus want us to have the Holy Spirit?"

Dean's answer was an emphatic "Of course!"

So Hank posited the question: "Then why haven't you and I asked for this gift?"

Dean rejoined with, "That's a good question!"

So Hank's invitation followed: "Come over to the house tonight and we'll ask to be immersed in the Holy Spirit! What do you say?"

Dean enthusiastically replied, "Great! I'll be there!"

Hank was praying when he heard the doorbell ring. He opened the door and welcomed his friend inside. "I was just praying and thinking about you."

Somewhat startled, Dean said, "Oh? What about?" Hank explained that he had wondered if they should wait to receive the Holy Spirit in Jedd's class. "No!" replied Dean. "I want to treat the receiving of the Father's gift as a 'special time' you and I can share. We've been friends a long time and we believe the same in everything the Lord has said in His Word, so let's do this together!"

Hank thought for a moment and agreed. "I feel the same, Dean, so let's get started!" They knelt on the floor and Hank began to pray:

"Father, You are such a Great God! When we look around, we see the beauty You have created and we are in awe! We see the mountains that You put in place and the trees in all their majesty ... the river that runs through our town and the stars that come out at night! You love us enough to share this with all of us! Dean and I are kneeling here to ask for the gift of the Holy Spirit. So, Holy Spirit, I ask that You come upon us tonight as You came upon the disciples on the Day of Pentecost. Fill us and baptize us in the name of Jesus! Amen."

There was a peaceful silence for a few minutes; both had their eyes closed. Then a faint sound was heard which got louder each passing moment. Hank realized it was coming from him! He didn't know what he was saying but it sounded beautiful! Could this be 'speaking-in-tongues' that the Bible talks about? They weren't sure, but they didn't want it to stop because something magnificent was happening! Then another voice was heard, not like Hank's but just as beautiful! It was Dean's voice and when Hank looked at his face, it was wet with tears (as was Hank's)! They continued to pray for a while until they were 'spent!'

They sat back against the couch and looked at the time: two hours had elapsed from when they began! It felt like just a few minutes, not two hours! Hank asked Dean if he was all right and he said, "I have never felt better!"

Hank said, "Dean! We were just baptized in the Holy Spirit!"

Dean regained some composure and said, "Yes, I know... I'm just overwhelmed! Hank, I think each of us needs to be alone with the Lord, so I'm going home because I have a place in my house that I use just to be with God."

Hank agreed and said, "OK, I'll see you tomorrow." Hank prayed in tongues for hours after Dean left, then fell asleep.

Hank was 35 years old when he asked Jesus to be Lord of his life. Since then, life had become better each year. Dean, on the other hand, grew up in a Christian home but never knew Jesus. His parents said they were Christian but never went to church or treated anyone as if they were Christian. It wasn't until Hank led him to Jesus that he became a Christian. Yesterday they were Baptized in the Holy Spirit together ... a day that will not be forgotten by them because of the majesty that they experienced. As friends, they have discussed the Lord many times but, for them, He never felt so close as they experienced on this special day! Speaking in this new language enables something unique to happen that can't be easily or fully explained. It simply draws one closer to the Lord.

As the days moved forward, Hank began to pray for people in need and the difficulties he experienced in the past were removed. Praying for others had become much easier. Hank even prayed for someone he didn't know exactly what to pray for, but now Hank can pray in this new language knowing God hears him because the Holy Spirit gives him 'the utterance'. What a wonderful way to live ... having the ability to speak directly to God with the help of the Holy Spirit! It's difficult to understand why anyone would refuse this powerful gift!

Not Special... Just Blessed

Hank went by the Church to say hello and to tell Jedd of his Baptism in the Holy Spirit. Of course Jedd was up on a ladder painting the Church. "Hey Jedd!" Hank said. "What's happening?" was Jedd's reply.

Hank said, "I want to tell you about what took place last night!"

"OK! I'll be right down." Jedd came down the ladder and sat with Hank on a small bench under a magnificent 'specimen' tree. Hank told him that the Holy Spirit baptized him and Dean last night! Jedd's excitement was effervescent: "I'm so pleased that you received this powerful gift! Now use it often ... even if you don't have anything you want from God. Use this often because it edifies you and that builds you up in the Lord!"

Hank said, "This is overwhelming! I can't believe this happened to me!" Jedd told him not to think that he is better than anyone else just because he was given this gift. That would be wrong because he was 'not special' … he was 'just blessed!'

Jedd finished his 'Church-painting-task' for the day, then went down to the homeless shelter and helped give out food and clothing to the needy. He visited the poor and the widows and even took time to go into the woods to distribute food and clothing. Hank sometimes can't get his head around what has taken place since the arrival of this 'old woodsman'. Their town is not the same and he thought back to when Dean and he had coffee together and spoke of how outstanding it would be to experience what the early Church had when it began. To say he is pleased to see the Holy Spirit at work in a town that needs Him so much is awe-inspiring! Hank knew now how thrilling it is to see prayers answered in such a divine way!

Before Hank knew it, the week was over and he found himself entering the Church for Sunday School Class. There's something very different about this class—a sense of excitement prevails, but it's a 'peaceful' excitement. Hank didn't know if he should say anything about what Dean and he experienced or whether he should wait for Jedd's lead?

Jedd began, "Now that we understand how much the Father and the Son want us to have the gift of the Holy Spirit (and what a powerful gift He is), let's start to talk about 'receiving' the gift of the Holy Spirit. Does anyone have any questions?"

"Yes!" someone yelled out. "Is the Holy Spirit for everyone?"

Jedd said, "Yes! It's meant for every believer but unfortunately not everyone will receive the gift; the reason for this is they don't really 'desire' it. They'll just 'accept' it if it's given but they're not in obedience to the commands of God. The Word is very clear about this: God wants you to 'desire' this gift with all your heart!

"When a person opens the door of his heart to the Lordship of Jesus, it's His Spirit that makes us new and perfect! This 'newness' is actually the re-birth by the Holy Spirit, thus the term 'Born Again'. Every true believer is 're-born' of the Spirit. As such, they have experienced the work of the Holy Spirit in a number of important ways: 'Conviction' and 'Regeneration' are some of the ways we've experienced the 'witness' of the Holy Spirit in our lives! Thus His Words throughout Scripture now enable us to readily accept that we are children of God! However, the magnitude of power that God wants for His children can only be reached through the Baptism in the Holy Spirit. It is God's will that every Christian be baptized in the Holy Spirit.

Acts 2:38-39
38 Peter said to them, "Repent, and be baptized, every one of you, in the name of Jesus Christ for the forgiveness of sins, and you will receive the gift of the Holy Spirit.
39 For the promise is to you, and to your children, and to all who are far off, even as many as the Lord our God will call to Himself."

Someone asked, "Is the Baptism of the Holy Spirit for today?"

Jedd replied, "Some say that the Baptism in the Holy Spirit is extinct, that it no longer exists today. Some approach it in another way and say that every 'born-again Christian' was baptized in the Spirit at his or her conversion. These 'pronouncements' or 'teachings' have the essence of deceiving the devoted of something very important that Christ provided for them as part of their essential inheritance in this life. The Word is very clear that the Baptism in the Spirit is not the same as 'regeneration'. It is important that we do not allow tradition, even 'evangelical tradition, to take a higher place than the Word of God in our doctrine and in our lives.

"I remember when I received the Holy Spirit; it took me six months before I received Him. I never gave up… I just pursued Him until this new language began. By the way, that's how you know you've received Him, you begin to speak in an unknown language."

Someone injected, "Can someone have the Holy Spirit without speaking in tongues?"

Jedd calmly replied, "No, the only evidence of receiving the Holy Spirit is speaking in an unknown language … that's what the Bible says. Why is this so difficult for people to understand? Speaking in an unknown language means that you are speaking directly to God and He is the only One who understands what is being said. Why is this so important? Because the evil one (your enemy) does not know what is being said, so he does not know how to come against you!"

Someone said, "That makes sense, so how do we receive the gift of the Holy Spirit?"

Jedd replied, "You ask God. Remember, you must 'desire' Him with all your heart. Who, among those of us here today, wants this gift right now?"

Many hands were raised. Jedd said, "OK, then I pray that each one of you would open your heart for Jesus to come in and be Lord of your life!" He then asked the Holy Spirit to baptize each one of them! Then he said, "God or the Holy Spirit will do His work and you must do yours by opening your mouth and begin to speak and let words flow from you."

Most began to speak in another language! Some needed a little more time, but all spoke in a new tongue! The joy was intoxicating! Little did Hank know, but one of the people who received the Holy Spirit was the pastor of their Church! So when the service began, he informed the entire congregation of his action and wanted all to know the wonderful gift of the Holy Spirit!

Someone called out, "Does this mean this Church will become a 'holy-roller' kind of Church?"

The pastor replied, "No! But it will mean that 'tongues' may break out in this Church at times and we will follow the Bible when it comes to that occurrence!"

CHAPTER SEVEN

THE HOLY SPIRIT AND SCRIPTURES

Sunday service began as usual except that a new and unique characteristic permeated the atmosphere. Everywhere you looked, the Holy Spirit could be seen on faces throughout the congregation! Service was full of praise and worship—especially from Jedd who still sang with the loudest voice you ever heard! Then the pastor began to give his sermon. "Those who went to Sunday school, that would be most of you, have experienced the Baptism of the Holy Spirit … me included! Let me give a little more background about this powerful gift. But, before I do, I want to explain a little about my walk with the Lord.

"I was raised in a good Christian home with parents who showed love to me in every way possible. They taught me the Word of God not only by using the Bible but also, also by their actions. The Holy Spirit was never talked about much in our home. When I went to school I received more insight on the Holy Spirit. When Jedd entered our lives he showed me more about the Holy Spirit then any book could teach me. The way he took over all the work around our Church building; the way he treated the homeless and the needy in town. So when the Sunday school teaching position opened up there was only one person who could fill that position that, of course, was Jedd. His teaching on the Holy Spirit was priceless. I want to tell you a little more about what I know.

"The Bible does give examples of some people who were baptized in the Spirit at the same time as their regeneration, but this is not always what happens. The Book of Acts reveals that repentance, Baptism in water, and the Baptism in the Holy Spirit, although all part of God's salvation plan, do not automatically happen in the same order all the time. It is interesting that, in Acts, where the Baptism in the Spirit happens to believers at the time of their conversion, the Bible puts emphasis on the fact that the apostles knew they were Baptized in the Spirit, "for they heard them speak with tongues and magnify God!" (Acts 10:46; and Acts 11:15-16).

Acts 10:46-47

46 For they heard them speaking in other languages and magnifying God. Then Peter answered,
47 "Can any man forbid the water, that these who have received the Holy Spirit as well as we, should not be Baptized?"

Acts 11:15-16

15 As I began to speak, the Holy Spirit fell on them, even as on us at the beginning.
16 I remembered the Word of the Lord, how He said, 'John indeed baptized in water, but you will be baptized in the Holy Spirit.'

"We certainly do not believe that speaking in a new tongue is the proof of being 'born again.' However, we can see that, consistently, it is the sign accompanying the New Testament Baptism in the Holy Spirit. It is important to state that every true, 'born-again' Christian has the Holy Spirit," Jedd emphasized as he quoted the Scriptures: 'Now if anyone does not have the Spirit of Christ, He (Christ) is not in him.'" (Romans 8:9; Acts 5:32)

Romans 8:9

9 But you are not in the flesh but in the Spirit, if it is so that the Spirit of God dwells in you. But if any man doesn't have the Spirit of Christ, he is not His. God gives the Holy Spirit 'to those who obey Him.'

Acts 5:32

32 We are His witnesses of these things; and so also is the Holy Spirit, whom God has given 'to those who obey Him.'

"To receive Christ is an act of obedience by which the person submits to the 'work of the cross' and becomes a new person."

2 Corinthians 5:17

17 Therefore if anyone is in Christ, he is a new creation. The old things have passed away. Behold, all things have become new.

"The apostles received the Holy Spirit in regeneration before the ascension when Jesus breathed on them and said, 'Receive the Holy Spirit!' (John 20:22). They were 'born again' of the Spirit through the resurrection of Jesus from the dead (1Peter 1:3; John 20:22). This was before the day of Pentecost. Jesus told them later to '...wait for the Promise of the Father in Jerusalem;' (Acts 1:4); '...for the Baptism in the Holy Spirit,' (Acts 1:5) after they had received the Spirit in regeneration. Therefore, in the case of the apostles, the Baptism in the Spirit and being 'Born of the Spirit' were two separate events. They were 'Born of the Spirit' in John 20:22 (as seen previously) before the Ascension, but were Baptized in the Spirit on the day of Pentecost...after the Ascension. It is important to note that only 'then' was the promise of Mark (16:17) fulfilled in the lives of the believers; for beginning at Pentecost '…they were all filled with the Holy Spirit and began to speak with other tongues, as the Spirit gave them utterance.'"

Acts 2:4; John 20:22
22 When He had said this, He breathed on them, and said to them, "Receive the Holy Spirit!"

1 Peter 1:3
3 Blessed are the God and Father of our Lord Jesus Christ, who according to His great mercy became our Father again to a living hope through the resurrection of Jesus Christ from the dead.

Acts 1:4
4 Being assembled together with them, He commanded them, "Don't depart from Jerusalem, but wait for the promise of the Father, which you heard from Me."

Acts 1:5
5 For John indeed baptized in water, but you will be baptized in the Holy Spirit not many days from now.

Mark 1:17
17 Jesus said to them, "Come after Me, and I will make you into fishers for men."

Acts 2:4
4 They were all filled with the Holy Spirit, and began to speak with other languages, as the Spirit gave them the ability to speak."

The pastor stopped and looked at the faces of those listening to him and said, "I know this a lot to digest and many scriptures to read over, so let's take the time to do that this week. I can't tell you what an important and life-changing event this is! I exhort you <u>not</u> to take it for granted!"

The service ended and Hank exited the Church as usual. He saw Dean and approached him and said, "Let's have coffee," and Dean agreed wholeheartedly! When they arrived at the coffee shop, they took their normal seats, but Hank noticed something 'different' about Dean. He was much happier than he had ever seen him before … and he seemed to be 'at peace.'

"Wow! You look different," Hank said.

"Yes, I'm very different. I love the way I feel … the new love I have for the Lord and my family and everyone that I see! I didn't think this could happen! It's just so extraordinary!"

Hank said, "I know, I feel the same emotions and I hope it never stops! Did you know that the Ephesian believers in Acts 19 were not 'true Christians' in the full sense of the word when Paul met them? They only knew of John's 'Water' Baptism of Repentance. They were not aware that the Holy Spirit had descended on those with the apostles. After Paul explained to them about Jesus' Resurrection, '…they were baptized in the name of the Lord Jesus Christ. When Paul had laid his hands on them, the Holy Spirit came upon them, and they spoke with other languages and prophesied.'"

Acts 19:5-6
5 When they heard this, they were baptized in the name of the Lord Jesus Christ.
6 When Paul had laid his hands on them, the Holy Spirit came upon them, and they spoke with other languages and prophesied.

Hank continued and said, "Here we see that Paul was interested in these disciples' relationship with the Holy Spirit. He showed them their need to be Baptized in water and the Holy Spirit. Again, 'speaking in tongues' is revealed to have accompanied this initial outpouring of the Holy Spirit upon the believers."

Dean was a little stunned and proclaimed, "There's so much about the Holy Spirit! I wonder why this information wasn't shown to me until now?"

Hank indicated that he was as perplexed about that as Dean. "It seems that this information could have been purposely hidden from us all these years," he replied.

Dean concluded by suggesting, "I guess we must leave the past alone or we may find a few people we would like to confront!"

That next week was full of excitement! The people of Hank's Church were out greeting the people of his town and telling them about Jesus. People were being saved and healed on the street and even in places like the hospital! It was sensational ... bordering on 'unbelievable!' Even the sun seemed more effervescent, it illuminated the environment, making it seem, for the first time, that their town was an 'out of the ordinary' kind of town, a town where people come to be 'blessed' and stay for the 'joy' they feel! The town 'glistened' because the Holy Spirit not only 'lived' in its people but also 'worked through their lives'—and, with that, everything changed!

CHAPTER EIGHT

WHO WE ARE IN JESUS CHRIST

Dean was quietly seated on a park bench next to the Church when Hank approached. "Hi Dean!"

He responded, "Hey, old friend! I know we wanted the power of the early Church to explode in our town, but I didn't expect Him so <u>fast</u> and so <u>inclusive</u>! I think I'll just sit back and watch the Holy Spirit do His work and enjoy every minute!"

Hank said, "I agree! I was just wondering... How can our Church sustain the commitment and the emotion that is happening all round town? You see how the surrounding towns are flooding our streets each weekend!"

Dean replied, "Of course, but that's what it's all about! We see our Church reaching people with the Gospel and healing them right on the street! Now that we have power to do miracles, they can't hold it in! This is 'hallelujah' time!"

Hank carried the thought further, saying, "Dean, I believe the reason we haven't experienced this sooner is because we don't know who we are in Christ."

Dean wondered, "What do you mean?"

Hank responded, "I don't know about you, but I notice that when we are asked 'who we are,' we might say, 'just a sinner saved by grace.' Although that was true at one time in my life, it doesn't apply to me now since I opened my heart to Jesus. I no longer see myself that way. Now when I'm asked, I say something like this: 'I'm the righteousness of God through Christ Jesus.' You see, you are not what <u>you</u> think you are, and it's not what <u>other</u> <u>people</u> think you are either. It's what <u>you</u> think <u>other</u> <u>people</u> think you are.

"One of the things I learned in this world is... Oh, how can I say this? Let me give you an illustration: suppose we're in a boat in the middle of the ocean. It's not the water that surrounds us that will make us drown, it's the water that comes <u>into</u> our boat that will make us drown. In other words, it's not what's 'said' around you that will hurt you, it's what's said that you 'let' come into your heart and mind that will hurt you. The Word says, '...therefore, don't let sin reign in your life.' It doesn't mean 'rain falling down,' it means 'reign' like 'control.' So you might say it this way: 'Do not let 'sin' control your life.'"

So Dean asked, "How do I do that?"

Hank responded, "You don't focus on the 'sin,' but you focus on what the 'Word' says you are! Here are just a few statements that I read as often as I can: 'Jesus on the cross obtained several 'rights' for us; such as, '...reign in life through the One, Jesus Christ.'"(Romans 5:17).

Romans 5:17
17 For if by the trespass of the one, death reigned through the one; so much more will those who receive the abundance of grace and of the gift of righteousness <u>reign in life through the One, Jesus Christ.</u>

"About this we are the righteousness of God in Jesus Christ."

2 Corinthians 5:21
21 For him who knew no sin He was made to be sin on our behalf; so that in him <u>we might become the righteousness of God</u>.

"I see what you mean," said Dean. "We are in Christ, so we get what we <u>don't deserve</u> instead of what we <u>do deserve</u>."

Hank followed with, "Yes! Dean, that's exactly right! I made a list of 'who we are in Christ.' Would you like to hear more?"

Dean exuded, "You bet!"

Hank began to enumerate: "I'm not looking at the things that <u>are</u> seen, but at the things which <u>are</u> <u>not</u> seen."

2 Corinthians 4:18
18 <u>while we don't look at the things which are seen, but at the things which are not seen</u>. For the things which are seen are temporal, but the things which are not seen are eternal.

Hank continued with, "I am casting down imaginations and every high thing that exalts itself against the knowledge of God."

2 Corinthians 10:5
5 <u>throwing down imaginations and every high thing that is exalted against the knowledge of God</u>, and bringing every thought into captivity to the obedience of Christ;

Hank then elaborated, "I am rooted and grounded in love, because Christ dwells within me."

Ephesians 3:17
17 that Christ may dwell in your hearts through faith; to the end that you, being rooted and grounded in love.

"Dean, that's just a portion of the scriptures that speak of 'who we are in Christ Jesus.' Dean said, "Hank, what should I do with this information?" Hank responded, "I don't know, but this is what I intend to do: I'm going to read these scriptures every day until I know them in my heart! I believe that, by doing this, I will become more aware of what Jesus accomplished on the Cross. When He said, 'It is finished,' He was saying that He had totally completed our salvation and taken away all the obstacles between us and God!"

Dean encouraged Hank to further explain that statement, so Hank continued, "Sure I will! When Jesus died on the cross, He died for all our sins— yesterdays, today's, and the sins we haven't committed yet. We now understand that when Jesus said, 'It is finished,' there were no more 'barriers' between God and us. Because of Jesus, we are sons and daughters of the living God! Because of Jesus, we have 'righteous standing' with God! Because of Jesus, we sit in 'heavenly places' in Christ Jesus! Because Jesus was separated from the Father, we will never be separated from the Father, ever again! Because His body was beaten and broken, we are healed! Because He shed His blood as the atonement for our sins, we are cleansed of all our sins! Jesus made us 'joint heirs' with Him! We have become 'adopted sons and daughters' of God!

"That's exciting because when you are born into a family, you are 'accepted' without anyone knowing how you will turn out! But when you are 'adopted', everyone sees your faults, but God accepts us anyway because of Jesus.

Dean said, "I never heard this before... What a revelation!"

And Hank summarized with, "I know! When I first read the scriptures that revealed these things to me, I was blown away! Dean, this is 'grace'! It's the grace Paul speaks about and the grace that will transform people, don't you agree? He gave us the gift of 'grace' and the gift of 'righteousness!'"

CHAPTER NINE

JEDD GOES BACK TO HIS CABIN

Jedd was finishing up some painting and general 'fix-up' at Ann's house and garage when Hank called to him. "Hey Jedd! Do you have a minute to talk?"

Jedd responded, "I Sure do!"

So Jedd and Hank sat on the grass nearby and Hank said, "Isn't it amazing what's happening in this town?"

Jedd concurred and said, "Yes! It certainly is, Hank! I didn't know exactly what I was to do when God sent me here."

Hank said, "You mean God sent you here?"

Jedd's reply was, "Yes! You see, God wanted to bless this little Church. However, the only way to receive the blessing God intended for you all was to receive the Holy Spirit! What's so surprising is how easily your Church welcomed the Holy Spirit! Truly, the blessings of God have fallen on this Church and will continue to fall as long as the Holy Spirit is kept alive in your minds and hearts! I'm so glad that you came by today because there's something that God wants from you and Dean. You see, no matter how 'enthusiastic' a Church has become in accepting the Holy Spirit, sometimes the congregation tends to 'forget' or 'fails to recall' just how much He did for them … <u>unless</u> someone reminds them and keeps the Holy Spirit prominent in their thoughts and actions! That's where you and Dean come in! The Lord wants you and Dean to be the ones who keep the Holy Spirit 'influential and noticeable'," Jedd, said.

Hank, caught off-guard, said, "I'm speechless! But that's your job!"

Jedd replied, "No Hank. I'll be leaving and returning to my cabin shortly and you and Dean will 'take up the mantle' of keeping the Holy Spirit 'alive and well' in your Church!"

Later on, Hank spoke to Dean about what Jedd had said. "That's a big commitment… Are we ready for it? I think we are! With the Holy Spirit's help, we can do anything! Remember! 'Greater is He who is within us…than he who is in the world!' Wasn't it our idea to ask the Lord to send us some help? Well, He did! Now we must carry it the rest of way!"

Dean inquired, "How do we accomplish this daunting task?"

Hank concluded: "First, we pray often in our 'spiritual language', and at the same time, learn everything we possibly can about the Holy Spirit."

It would be Sunday in few days and it was to be Jedd's last Sunday before he headed back home. Of course, the Church planned a going-away party. It would be a BIG party, undoubtedly the biggest this town had ever seen! Most likely a few streets would be blocked off to accommodate all the people that would be coming. It was all planned but something happened that changed everything! Jedd disappeared! No one could find him anywhere! What could have happened to him?

Someone said, "He must have gone home early. Would he do something like that?"

Hank said, "I don't know. Let's check out Ann's place where he lives."

So a few of the Church members went to his room above the garage and, when they arrived, they noticed a note attached to the inside of his door. It read something like this: "I thought it would be better if I went home early, for my journey is long and hard. I hope all of you know just how much I love you ... and how much I loved telling you about the Holy Spirit! Goodbye and enjoy your new life in the Holy Spirit! God's richest blessings to you all, Jedd."

Jedd was last seen walking north on Highway 101. He was praying as he made his way home and thanking the Lord for allowing him to have such a glorious experience! He heard the voice of the Lord saying, "Jedd, it is I who want to thank you for being so obedient. You accomplished all I had you do. Look for blessings in your days ahead." Jedd was overwhelmed and praised the Lord all the way home! He went the same way as he came, but this time the journey was a little easier ... for he walked with God.

The pastor came to Hank and Dean and asked if they would take over the Sunday school. They looked at each other and said, almost together, "We'd love to! So when do we start?"

The pastor said, "How about the beginning of next month?" Both Hank and Dean thought that would be perfect.

"OK then, it's set," confirmed the pastor. "Our town is getting bigger each week. People are coming on the weekends from towns that surround us, and the spirit of our Church is alive! People are giving their lives to the Lord and are being healed in ways that can only be described as 'miraculous'! Our Church is growing so that we need to expand. Our Sunday school has grown so much that we had to move it to the sanctuary—and even <u>that</u> is not able to hold all who are showing up! Could this be the revival that we've been hoping for and praying about? If this is not the beginning of a revival, then I can't explain what is happening here! If this is how the Christian Church began, then I can understand why people were joining that early Church and were willing to die for the Lord!"

Hank speaks to Dean often and both are filled with excitement! The Lord is definitely using them to touch the lives of families, their neighbors, and even people they meet for the first time. They are truly joyful and they just can't stop praising the Lord!

Epilogue

The craving for the Lord to 'move' in their town (as He did when He started His Church) came from a desire to see the power of God. Dean and Hank knew that God was the same today as He was back then. The Lord told His disciples that if they "…don't believe the words that I say, then believe in the signs and wonders that I perform." In essence, when we preach the Word, 'signs and wonders' should follow. You see, what makes the Christian Church 'different' from the world is the demonstration of God's power. The Church today does not demonstrate power at all. If you compare the Church with the world, you will find very little difference. When a person in the world is sick, he or she runs to a doctor and follows whatever the doctor says. Well, doesn't the Church do the same thing? What about when people or institutions in the world get into financial difficulties? They go to a financial counselor or a bank to help or lend them money. Well, doesn't the Church do the same thing? So we ask, "What should the Church do?" We should 'consult with and follow' the directives of the Lord our God.

The very 'first step' in finding solutions to the problems or 'challenges' is to know 'who we are in Christ Jesus!' What I mean is, Christ died on a cross and paid the price we could not pay. In so doing, He gave us a 'divine position' in Himself (as we covered in Chapter Six … and those were just a few of the scriptures that describe our position as 'believers'). If one 'takes up the challenge' and finds all the scriptures that describe our position in Jesus, one will notice that our Lord didn't just 'die' to save us from our sins, He did so much more! You see, He made us 'adopted sons and daughters' of God and, therefore, 'joint heirs' with Jesus! That means we have the same 'benefits' as Jesus!

We see ourselves as '…sinners saved by grace,' constantly worried about 'sinning', feeling bad and thinking we aren't worth much at all; God doesn't see us that way! When we were 'born again,' we became 'new creations' and that's how God sees us! He sees the 'new man or woman' instead of the 'old man or woman' who has passed away! Our 'new man or woman' is as 'perfect' as he or she will ever be! The 'old man or woman' will perish and the flesh that tempts them daily will no longer exist. So how do we become the new man or woman that God sees when He looks upon us?

Understand that we can't accomplish anything to achieve salvation because Jesus did it all! What gets us in trouble is that we think we must be 'good' and never sin. What we don't realize is that we can't stop sinning as long as we live in the flesh. God knew that we don't have what it takes 'not' to sin, so He made that provision for us! He sent His Son to eliminate the 'consequences' for sin. In essence, He took 'sin' out of the equation! I know this sounds somewhat like a 'fantasy' but it is not! Another way to say this is: once we are 'saved,' we are always saved! Many theologians will say, "That's ridiculous!" Ok then, under this reasoning, when 'sin happens,' do we lose our salvation? If that's true, does that mean we have to be born again … and again … and again? Does that mean we must be 'born again' several times during our lifetime?

Some may say, "No, we just have to confess our sins to God and He forgives us!" Let's look at this in the proper way: God the Father poured out His anger on His Son. The Word of God is very explicit, it says that the punishment for sin has been satisfied! God cannot punish that sin again. The price has already been paid!

Let's be very clear about this: when we sin, we must 'repent' or 'turn away' from sin and run back to Jesus! Sin must be 'hated' as much as God hates it! Sin opens the door to the enemy and gives him the ability to make our lives miserable. So, as believers, we must do all we can to stay as close to Jesus as is humanly possible! We are not to focus our attention on our sins! That will only drive us to sin more. Instead, we are to focus on Jesus and when we do, we will become more like Him every day! Remember that whatever we think about, focus on or give all our attention to is what we will become! So, we are to look at our Savior and see the beauty and omnipotence in Him! That's what God intended when He put His plan into action!

God put all His frustration and anger for sin on His Son and now He wants to show us as "...His people, called by His Name [Christians...believers...see 2 Chron. 7:14]..." that His love is 'boundless' and 'everlasting' ... just as He wanted when he created Adam and Eve! His consummate desire is to eliminate any barrier whatsoever between Him and us. It doesn't make any sense to keep or bear the consequences of sin; so He made us, His children, as 'complete as possible' in Jesus. He said that when we believe in His Son, He remembers our sin no more!

After Jesus left the earth, He sent us the Holy Spirit to teach us all about Him (Jesus) and show us His 'truths'. The Holy Spirit gives us the power not only to live for Him, but enables us to tell others all about what He and what His Father did for us on the Cross! Without the Holy Spirit, it is impossible to do anything worthwhile for God!

That's why Dean and Hank prayed for months that the Holy Spirit would come to their small town. The Holy Spirit did come to their town, not like He did in their neighboring town of Berry, Oregon. The experience of their town was a continuation of the town of Berry. Their town's experience was much better, however, because He came upon all of their townsfolk! He did His work through them and miracles happened with a demonstration of power! Their Church became 'full of grace' and they took that grace and transformed their town! They were 'truly blessed' and He took them to places that they never thought they could reach! Jedd came as God's 'ambassador'. Jedd was told by God to go to this small town and lead them to the Holy Spirit. Jedd came with his knowledge of the Holy Spirit and he demonstrated the Spirit with the work he did around their Church, at Ann's home, his visits to the homeless around town, and, of course, his teachings in their Bible Class. How 'exhilarating' and 'transformational' it was to see a demonstration of the Spirit of God!

Your Church could also experience the Holy Spirit! It would take a 'willingness' to pray for as long as it takes. As a leader, you must be a 'believer' and be 'filled with the Holy Spirit' in order to 'set the example'! Then you and others in your congregation … in your neighborhoods … in your city … would see the demonstration of God's Love that your eyes have yet to behold!

ABOUT THE AUTHOR

Phil was born in Brooklyn, New York, in the early 1940s, as Philip Sante Beckinella, to a middle-income family. He struggled through most of his schooling years. School became so much of a burden that he enlisted at seventeen into the U.S. Army and served for 3 years (at which time he obtained his High School Diploma). On his return from Baumholder, Germany, he continued his education and set a foot into the profession of architecture. Soon after his graduation, he was welcomed into one of New York's finest architectural firms. His talent allowed him to participate in design and production documents. He had a hand in the designing and constructing of hospitals from New York to California where he re-established his residence and has lived since 1974. He is now retired and living in the beautiful state of Oregon with his lovely wife, Sandra. His first adventure in writing was a short story called *The Visitor*. He's also completed a new book called *Can You Hear The Holy Spirit?*

Why would a man from such a background want to write? I guess we can say he's had a dormant but deep-seated desire to write; or there is something in him that just had to come out! While all that is true, that's not the 'real reason' he took up writing. You see, it was God's abiding love that drove him to write this story! It's the need for each and every Christian to know that there is a 'gift' from God the Father that they have yet to embrace, and without that gift, they seem to be left 'powerless'. So the work of the Church is not being done, as it should be. The power they need is available but is being left 'unused'. The unfortunate result is that many will 'lose out' on the wonderful and miraculous things Jesus bestowed to us when He paid the price for our salvation and freedom by His magnanimous, almost incomprehensible, sacrifice on the Cross.

Who We Are In Jesus Christ

RIGHTEOUSNESS

For if by the one man's offense, death reigned through the one, much more those who receive abundance of grace and of the gift of righteousness will reign in life through the One, Jesus Christ. - Romans 5:17

For He made Him who knew no sin to be sin for us, that we might become the righteousness of God in Him. - 2 Corinthians 5:21

...that I may gain Christ and be found in Him, not having my own righteousness, which is from the law, but that which is through faith in Christ, the righteousness which is from God by faith; that I may know Him and the power of His resurrection... - Philippians 3:8-10

But to him who does not work but believes on Him who justifies the ungodly, his faith is accounted for righteousness, just as David also describes the blessedness of the man to whom God imputes righteousness apart from works. - Romans 4:5,6

For the promise that he would be the heir of the world was not to Abraham or to his seed through the law, but through the righteousness of faith. - Romans 4:13

...so that as sin reigned in death, even so grace might reign through righteousness to eternal life through Jesus Christ our Lord.
- Romans 5:21

Fear not, for I am with you; be not dismayed, for I am your God. I will strengthen you, yes, I will help you, I will uphold you with My righteous right hand. - Isaiah 41:10

For what does the Scripture say? "Abraham believed God, and it was accounted to him for righteousness." - Romans 4:3

For You, O Lord, will bless the righteous; with favor You will surround him as with a shield.
- Psalm 5:12

Many are the afflictions of the righteous, but the Lord delivers him out of them all.
- Psalm 34:19

"But seek first the kingdom of God and His righteousness, and all these things shall be added to you. - Matthew 6:33

Treasures of wickedness profit nothing, but righteousness delivers from death. The Lord will not allow the righteous soul to famish, but He casts away the desire of the wicked.
- Proverbs 10:2,3

Blessings are on the head of the righteous, but violence covers the mouth of the wicked. The memory of the righteous is blessed, but the name of the wicked will rot.
- Proverbs 10:6,7

The labor of the righteous leads to life, the wages of the wicked to sin. - Proverbs 10:16

The fear of the wicked will come upon him, and the desire of the righteous will be granted.
- Proverbs 10:24

The hope of the righteous will be gladness, but the expectation of the wicked will perish.
- Proverbs 10:28

The righteous will never be removed, but the wicked will not inhabit the earth.
- Proverbs 10:30

In the way of righteousness is life, and in its pathway there is no death.
- Proverbs 12:28

Evil pursues sinners, but to the righteous, good shall be repaid. A good man leaves an inheritance to his children's children, but the wealth of the sinner is stored up for the righteous. - Proverbs 13:21,22

The righteous eats to the satisfying of his soul, but the stomach of the wicked shall be in want. - Proverbs 13:25

The righteous is delivered from trouble, and it comes to the wicked instead. - Proverbs 11:8

Though they join forces, the wicked will not go unpunished; but the posterity of the righteous will be delivered. - Proverbs 11:21
-

I am reigning in life by Jesus Christ. - Romans 5:17

I am the righteousness of God in Christ Jesus. - 3 Corinthians 5:21

I am rooted and grounded in love, because Christ dwells within me. - Ephesians 3:17

I am the workmanship of God, created in Christ Jesus for good works. - Ephesians 2:10

I am a partaker of God's divine nature. - 2 Peter 1:4

I am prosperous and in good health, because my soul prospers. - 3 John 1:2

I am being transformed by the renewing of my mind to prove the perfect will of God. - Romans 12:2

I am a temple of the Holy Ghost. - 1 Corinthians 6:19

I am given exceedingly great and precious promises, and by them I partake of the divine nature, having escaped the corruption that is in the world through lust. - 2 Peter 1:4

I am led by the spirit of God; therefore, I am a son of God - Romans 8:14 ...

I am not walking after the flesh, but after the Spirit. - Romans 8:1 ...

FAITH

And not being weak in faith, he did not consider his own body, already dead (since he was about a hundred years old), and the deadness of Sarah's womb. He did not waver at the promise of God through unbelief, but was strengthened in faith, giving glory to God, and being fully convinced that what He had promised He was also able to perform.
- Romans 4:19,20

Let us hold fast the confession of our hope without wavering, for He who promised is faithful.
- Hebrews 10:23

By faith Sarah herself also received strength to conceive seed, and she bore a child when she was past the age, because she judged Him faithful who had promised.
- Hebrews 11:11

Now faith is the substance of things hoped for, the evidence of things not seen.
- Hebrews 11:1

So shall My word be that goes forth from My mouth; it shall not return to Me void, but it shall accomplish what I please, and it shall prosper in the thing for which I sent it.   - Isaiah 55:11

"God is not a man, that He should lie, nor a son of man, that He should repent. Has He said, and will He not do? Or has He spoken, and will He not make it good?
- Numbers 23:19

Forever, O Lord, Your word is settled in heaven. - Psalm 119:89

"Blessed be the Lord, who has given rest to His people Israel, according to all that He promised. There has not failed one word of all His good promise, which He promised through His servant Moses. -1 Kings 8:56

"For assuredly, I say to you, whoever says to this mountain, 'Be removed and be cast into the sea,' and does not doubt in his heart, but believes that those things he says will be done, he will have whatever he says.
- Mark 11:23

"Therefore I say to you, whatever things you ask when you pray, believe that you receive them, and you will have them. - Mark 11:24

For we walk by faith, not by sight.
- 2 Corinthians 5:7

For in Christ Jesus neither circumcision nor un-circumcision avails anything, but faith working through love.   -
Galatians 5:6

...God, who gives life to the dead and calls those things which do not exist as though they did; - Romans 4:17

Jesus Christ is the same yesterday, today, and forever. - Hebrews 13:8

I am not looking at the things that are seen, but at the things which are not seen. - 2 Corinthians 4:18

I am casting down imaginations and every high thing that exalts itself against the knowledge of God... - 2 Corinthians 10:5...

HEALTH AND HEALING

But He was pierced for our rebellion, crushed for our sins. He was beaten so we could be whole. He was whipped so we could be healed. - Isaiah 53:5

Who Himself bore our sins in His own body on the tree, that we, having died to self, might live for righteousness--by whose stripes you were healed. - 1 Peter 2:24

But if the Spirit of Him who raised Jesus from the dead dwells in you, He who raised Christ from the dead will also give life to your mortal bodies through His Spirit who dwells in you. - Romans 8:11

He who did not spare His own Son, but delivered Him up for us all, how shall He not with Him also freely give us all things?
- Romans 8:32

Suddenly, a man with leprosy approached Him and knelt before Him. The man said, "Lord, if You are willing, You can heal me and make me clean." Jesus reached out and touched him. He said, "I am willing; be healed!" And instantly the leprosy disappeared. - Matthew 8:2,3…

"Lord, help!" They cried in their trouble, and He saved them from their distress. He sent out His word and healed them, snatching them from the door of death.   -
Psalm 107:19,20

For He will rescue you from every trap and protect you from deadly disease. - Psalm 91:3

He also brought them out with silver and gold, and there was none feeble among His tribes. - Psalm 105:37

Beloved, I pray that in all respects, you may prosper and be in good health, just as your soul prospers. - 3 John 1:2

"The thief does not come except to steal, and to kill, and to destroy. I have come that they may have life, and that they may have it more abundantly." - John 10:10

Do not be afraid of the terrors of the night, nor the arrow that flies in the day. Do not dread the disease that stalks in darkness, nor the disaster that strikes at midday. Though a thousand fall at your side, though ten thousand are dying around you, these evils will not touch you. - Psalm 91:5-7

"With long life I will satisfy him, and show him My salvation" - Psalm 91:16

"…I am the Lord who heals you."   - Exodus 15:26

"...I will give you back our heath and heal our wounds," says the Lord.
- Jeremiah 30:17

Bless the Lord, O my soul, and forget not all His benefits: Who forgives all your iniquities, who heals all your disease - Psalm 103:2,3

My son, give attention to my words; incline your ear to my sayings. Do not let them depart from your eyes; keep them in the midst of your heart; for they are life to those who find them, and health to all their flesh.
- Proverbs 4:20-22

And Jesus went about all Galilee, teaching in their synagogues, preaching the gospel of the kingdom, and healing all kinds of sickness and all kinds of disease among the people.   - Matthew 4:23

News about Him spread as far as Syria, and people soon began bringing to Him all who were sick. And whatever their sickness or disease, or if they were demon-possessed or epileptic or paralyzed, he healed them all.
- Matthew 4:24

When Jesus had entered Capernaum, a centurion came to him asking for help and said, "Lord, my servant lies at my home paralyzed and in terrible suffering!" Jesus said to him, "I will go and heal him."
- Matthew 8: 5-7

When evening had come, they brought to Him many who were demon-possessed. And He cast out the spirits with a word, and healed all who were sick, that it might be fulfilled which was spoken by Isaiah the prophet, saying: "He Himself took our infirmities and bore our sicknesses." - Matthew 8:16,17

Then Jesus turned to the paralyzed man and said, "Stand up, pick up your mat, and go home!" And the man jumped up and went home! - Matthew 9:6

Then great multitudes came to Him, having with them the lame, blind, mute, maimed, and many others; and they laid them down at Jesus' feet, and He healed them.   -
Matthew 15:30

So Jesus had compassion on them and touched their eyes. Immediately they received their sight and followed Him.   - Matthew 20:34

Jesus stood still, and said, "Call him." They called the blind man; saying to him, "Cheer up! Get up. He is calling you! "He, casting away his cloak, sprang up, and came to Jesus. Jesus asked him, "What do you want me to do for you?" The blind man said to him, "Rabboni, that I may see again."

Jesus said to him, "Go your way. Your faith has made you well." Immediately he received his sight, and followed Jesus on the way.

- Mark 10:49-52 …

When the sun was setting, all those who had any
that were sick with various diseases brought them
to Him; and He laid His hands on every one of
them and healed them.
- Luke 4:40

And the whole multitude sought to touch Him, for
power went out from Him and healed them all. -
Luke 6:19

A funeral procession was coming out as He
approached the village gate. The young man who
had died was a widow's only son, and a large
crowd from the village was with her. When the
Lord saw her, His heart overflowed with
compassion. "Do not cry." He said. Then He
walked over to the coffin and touched it, and the
bearers stopped. "Young man," He said, "I tell
you, get up!" Then the dead boy sat up and began
to talk! And Jesus gave him back to his mother.
- Luke 7:12-15

And behold, there was a woman who had been
crippled by a spirit for eighteen years. She was
bent over and could not straighten up at all. When
Jesus saw her He called her forward and said to
her, "Woman, you are set free from your
infirmity." Then He put His hands on her, and
immediately she straightened up and praised God.
- Luke 13:11-13

"God anointed Jesus of Nazareth with the Holy

Spirit and with power, who went about doing good and healing all who were oppressed by the devil, for God was with Him." -
Acts 10:38

PRAYER FOR HEALING AND WHOLENESS

"Lord Jesus, I thank You that You love me and that You are both able and willing to heal me. At the cross, You took all my sicknesses and pains in Your own body, and by Your stripes I am healed! Your body was scourged and broken so that mine can be made whole. I receive all that You have done for me and I rest in Your finished work. There is nothing more for me to do. As I wait on You for the complete manifestation of my healing, I choose to focus on and give praise for Your great love for me. Amen!"

FAVOR

For You, O Lord, will bless the righteous; with favor You will surround him as with a shield.
- Psalm 5:12

You prepare a table before me in the presence of my enemies; You anoint my head with oil; my cup runs over. Surely goodness and mercy shall follow me all the days of my life; and I will dwell in the house of the Lord forever. For His anger is but for a moment, His favor is for life; weeping may endure for a night, but joy comes in the morning. - Psalm 30:5

"The Lord make His face shine upon you, and be gracious to you; the Lord lift up His countenance upon you, and give you peace."
- Numbers 6:25,26

And his master saw that the Lord was with him and that the Lord made all he did to prosper in his hand. So Joseph found favor in his sight, - Genesis 39:3,4

You have granted me life and favor, and Your care has preserved my spirit. - Job 10:12

Who redeems your life from destruction, Who crowns you with loving kindness and tender mercies, Who satisfies your mouth with good things, so that your youth is renewed like the eagle's. - Psalm 103:4,5

For I know the thoughts that I think toward you, says the Lord, thoughts of peace and not of evil, to give you a future and a hope.
- Jeremiah 29:11

"And the glory which You gave Me I have given them, that they may be one just as We are one: I in them, and You in Me; that they may be made perfect in one, and that the world may know that You have sent Me, and have loved them as You have loved Me."
- John 17:22-23

So continuing daily with one accord in the temple, and breaking bread from house to house, they ate their food with gladness and simplicity of heart, praising God and having favor with all the people. And the Lord added to the church daily those who were being saved. - Acts 2:46-47

"Call to Me, and I will answer you, and show you great and mighty things, which you do not know."
- Jeremiah 33:3

For if by the one man's offense many died, much more the grace of God and the gift by the grace of the one Man, Jesus Christ, abounded to many. - Romans 5:15

For sin shall not have dominion over you, for you are not under law but under grace.
- Romans 6:14

For if by the one man's offense death reigned

through the one, much more those who receive abundance of grace and of the gift of righteousness will reign in life through the One, Jesus Christ. - Romans 5:17

For you know the grace of our Lord Jesus Christ, that though He was rich, yet for your sakes He became poor, that you through His poverty might become rich.
- 2 Corinthians 8:9

And God is able to make all grace abound toward you, that you, always having all sufficiency in all things, may have an abundance for every good work.
- 2 Corinthians 9:8

Blessed be the God and Father of our Lord Jesus Christ, who has blessed us with every spiritual blessing in the heavenly places in Christ, - Ephesians 1:3

In Him we have redemption through His blood, the forgiveness of sins, according to the riches of His grace, which He made to abound toward us in all wisdom and prudence,
- Ephesians 1:7,8

Now may our Lord Jesus Christ Himself, and our God and Father, who has loved us and given us everlasting consolation and good hope by grace, comfort your hearts and establish you in every good word and work.
- 2 Thessalonians 2:16-17

And the grace of our Lord was exceedingly abundant, with faith and love, which are in Christ Jesus. - 1 Timothy 1:14

Let us therefore come boldly to the throne of grace, that we may obtain mercy and find grace to help in time of need.
- Hebrews 4:16

PROSPERITY

"For to everyone who has, more shall be given, and he will have abundance; but from the one who does not have, even what he does have shall be taken away." -
Matthew 25:29 …

Let them shout for joy and rejoice, who favor my vindication; and let them say continually, "The LORD be magnified, Who delights in the prosperity of His servant."
- Psalm 35:27 …

Beloved, I pray that in all respects you may prosper and be in good health, just as your soul prospers - 3 John 1:2 …

He will be like a tree firmly planted by streams of water, which yields its fruit in its season and its leaf does not wither; and in whatever he does, he prospers. - Psalm 1:3

But you shall remember the LORD your God, for it is He who is giving you power to make wealth, that He may confirm His covenant which He swore to your fathers, as it is this day. - Deuteronomy 8:18

A rich man's wealth is his strong city, and like a high wall in his own imagination.
- Proverbs 18:11

Do not trust in oppression and do not vainly hope

in robbery; if riches increase, do not set your heart upon them. - Psalm 62:10

And my God shall supply all your need according to His riches in glory by Christ Jesus. - Philippians 4:19

For you know the grace of our Lord Jesus Christ, that though He was rich, yet for your sake He became poor, so that you through His poverty might become rich.
- 2 Corinthians 8:9

The Lord will command the blessing upon you in your barns and in all that you put your hand to, and He will bless you in the land which the Lord your God gives you.   -
Deuteronomy 28:8

It will be healing to your body and refreshment to your bones. Honor the LORD from your wealth and from the first of all your produce;
- Proverbs 3:8-9

And my God will supply all your needs according to His riches in glory in Christ Jesus.
- Philippians 4:19

Now He who supplies seed to the sower and bread for food will supply and multiply your seed for sowing   and increase the harvest of your righteousness;

11 you will be enriched in everything for all liberality, which through us is producing thanksgiving to God. - 2 Corinthians 9:10-11

He who did not spare His own Son, but delivered Him over for us all, how will He not also with Him freely give us all things?   - Romans 8:32

And God is able to make all grace abound to you, so that   always having all sufficiency   in everything, you may have an abundance for every good deed; - 2 Corinthians 9:8

Be anxious for nothing, but in everything by prayer and supplication, with thanksgiving, let your requests be made known to God. 7 And the peace of God, which surpasses all comprehension, will guard your hearts and your minds in Christ Jesus. - Philippians 4:6-7

This is the confidence, which we have before Him, that if we ask anything according to His will, He hears us. 15 And if we know that He hears us in whatever we ask, we know that we have the requests, which we have asked from Him. - 1 John 5:14-15

Beloved, I pray that in all respects you may prosper and be in good health, just as your soul prospers. - 3 John 1:2

Therefore let us draw near with confidence to the throne of grace, so that we may receive mercy and find grace to help in time of need.   - Hebrews 4:16

Do not worry then, saying, 'What will we eat?' or 'What will we drink?' or 'What will we wear for clothing?' 32 For the Gentiles eagerly seek all these things; for your heavenly Father knows that you need all these things. - Matthew 6:31-32
…

If you then, being evil, now how to give good gifts to your children, how much more will your Father who is in heaven give good things to those who ask Him - Matthew 7:11

The name of the Lord is a strong tower; the righteous run to it and are safe.
- Proverbs 18:10

You are my hiding place; You shall preserve me from trouble; You shall surround me with songs of deliverance.
- Psalm 32:7

How precious is Your loving kindness, O God! Therefore the children of men put their trust under the shadow of Your wings.
- Psalm 36:7

The fear of man brings a snare, but whoever trusts in the Lord shall be safe.
- Proverbs 29:25

For God has not given us a spirit of fear, but of power and of love and of a sound mind.
- 2 Timothy 1:7

...For He Himself has said, "I will never leave you nor forsake you." So we may boldly say: "The Lord is my helper; I will not fear. What can man do to me?"
- Hebrews 13:5,6

I will both lie down in peace, and sleep; for You alone, O Lord, make me dwell in safety.
- Psalm 4:8

As for God, His way is perfect; the word of the Lord is proven; He is a shield to all who trust in Him.
- Psalm 18:30

You shall hide them in the secret place of Your presence from the plots of man; You shall keep them secretly in a pavilion from the strife of tongues.
- Psalm 31:20

But let all those rejoice who put their trust in You; let them ever shout for joy, because You defend them; let those also who love Your name be joyful in You.
- Psalm 5:11

The Lord will preserve him and keep him alive, and he will be blessed on the earth; You will not deliver him to the will of his enemies.
- Psalm 41:2

Be merciful to me, O God, be merciful to me! For my soul trusts in You; and in the shadow of Your wings I will make my refuge, until these calamities have passed by.
- Psalm 57:1

"Then the trees of the field shall yield their fruit, and the earth shall yield her increase. They shall be safe in their land; and they shall know that I am the Lord, when I have broken the bands of their yoke and delivered them from the hand of those who enslaved them."
- Ezekiel 34:27

He has delivered us from the power of darkness and conveyed us into the kingdom of the Son of His love, in whom we have redemption through His blood, the forgiveness of sins.
- Colossians 1:13-14

The LORD will command the blessing upon you in your barns and in all that you put your hand to, and He will bless you in the land which the LORD your God gives you - Deuteronomy 28:8

It will be healing to your body and refreshment to your bones. Honor the LORD from your wealth and from the first of all your produce;   - Proverbs 3:8-9

And my God will supply your needs according to His riches in glory in Christ Jesus.   - Philippians 4:19

Now He who supplies seed to the sower and bread for food will supply and multiply your seed for sowing and increase the harvest of your righteousness; you will be enriched in everything for all liberality, which through us is producing thanksgiving to God. - 2 Corinthians 9:10-11

He who did not spare His own Son, but delivered Him over for us all, how will He not also with Him freely give us all things? - Romans 8:32

And God is able to make all grace abound to you, so that always having all sufficiency in everything, you may have an abundance for every good deed; - 2 Corinthians 9:8

6 Be anxious for nothing, but in everything by prayer and supplication with thanksgiving let your requests be made known to God.
7 And the peace of God, which surpasses all comprehension, will guard your hearts and your minds in Christ Jesus. - Philippians 4:6-7

This is the confidence, which we have before Him, that, if we ask anything according to His will, He hears us. And if we know that He hears us in whatever we ask, we know that we have the requests, which we have asked from Him.   -1 John 5:14-15

Beloved, I pray that in all respects you may prosper and be in good health, just as your soul prospers. - 3 John 1:2

Therefore let us draw near with confidence to the throne of grace, so that we may receive mercy and find grace to help in time of need.   - Hebrews 4:16

Do not worry then, saying, 'What will we eat?' or 'What will we drink?' or 'What will we wear for clothing?' For the Gentiles eagerly seek all these things; for your heavenly Father knows that you need all these things - Matthew 6:31-32

If you then, being evil, know how to give good gifts to your children, how much more will your Father who is in heaven give what is good to those who ask Him! - Matthew 7:11

The name of the Lord is a strong tower; the righteous run to it and are safe. - Proverbs 18:10

You are my hiding place; You shall preserve me from trouble; You shall surround me with songs of deliverance. - Psalm 32:7

How precious is Your loving kindness, O God! Therefore the children of men put their trust under the shadow of Your wings.- Psalm 36:7

The fear of man brings a snare, but whoever trusts in the Lord shall be safe. - Proverbs 29:25

For God has not given us a spirit of fear, but of power and of love and of a sound mind.   - 2 Timothy 1:7

...For He Himself has said,? Will never leave you nor forsake you. So we may boldly say:? The Lord is my helper; I will not fear. What can man do to me?" - Hebrews 13:5

I will both lie down in peace, and sleep; for You alone, O Lord, make me dwell in safety.   - Psalm 4:8

As for God, His way is perfect; the word of the Lord is proven; He is a shield to all who trust in Him. - Psalm 18:30

You shall hide them in the secret place of Your presence from the plots of man; You shall keep them secretly in a pavilion from the strife of tongues. - Psalm 31:20

But let all those rejoice who put their trust in You; let them ever shout for joy, because You defend them; let those also who love Your name be joyful in You. - Psalm 5:11

The Lord will preserve him and keep him alive, and he will be blessed on the earth; You will not deliver him to the will of his enemies.   - Psalm 41:2

Be merciful to me, O God, be merciful to me! For my soul trusts in You; and in the shadow of Your wings I will make my refuge, until these calamities have passed by. - Psalm 57:1

Then the trees of the field shall yield their fruit, and the earth shall yield her increase. They shall be safe in their land; and they shall know that I am the Lord, when I have broken the bands of their yoke and delivered them from the hand of those who enslaved them - Ezekiel 34:27

He has delivered us from the power of darkness and conveyed us into the kingdom of the Son of His love, in whom we have redemption through His blood, the forgiveness of sins.   - Colossians 1:134

www.ingramcontent.com/pod-product-compliance
Lightning Source LLC
Chambersburg PA
CBHW070641030426
42337CB00020B/4111